TOWARD A
FILM
HUMANISM

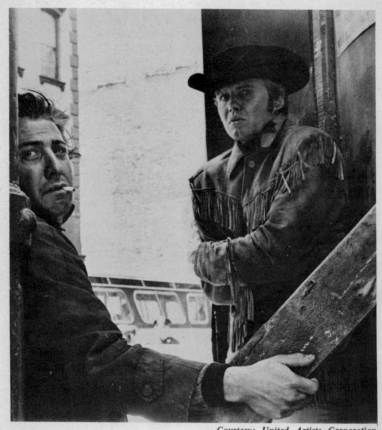

Jon Voigt and Dustin Hoffman in *Midnight Cowboy.*

TOWARD A
FILM
HUMANISM

(originally titled *Theology Through Film*)

Neil P. Hurley

A DELTA BOOK

FOR MY MOTHER

A DELTA BOOK
Published by
Dell Publishing Co., Inc.
1 Dag Hammarskjold Plaza
New York, New York 10017

*The author wishes to acknowledge the permission
granted by Warner Bros. Inc. to reproduce a film still
from the motion picture* REBEL WITHOUT A CAUSE
*copyright © 1955 by Warner Bros. Pictures, Inc.; from
the motion picture* WHO'S AFRAID OF VIRGINIA WOOLF
*copyright © 1965 by Warner Bros. Pictures, Inc.; from
the motion picture* WOODSTOCK *copyright © 1970 by
Warner Bros. Inc.; from the motion picture* THE DAMNED
copyright © 1969 by Warner Bros.–Seven Arts, Inc.

*The author wishes to acknowledge with gratitude the
cooperation of The Museum of Modern Art/Film Stills
Archives, The Memory Shop of New York City, The
National Catholic Office for Motion Pictures, and The
New York Public Library Picture Collection for aid
in obtaining film stills for this volume.*

Delta ® TM 755118, Dell Publishing Co., Inc.

Reprinted by arrangement with the Author.

Printed in the United States of America

First Delta printing—April 1975

Contents

"Quo universalius, eo divinius!"

Preface

Movies are for the masses what theology is for an elite. In this generalization is found the motive for this book. For nowhere is the distance between technics and thought so pronounced as between those who provide what *Time* once called "those celluloid fables which feed the dreams of the world" and those engaged in what the medieval schoolman St. Anselm called "faith in search of understanding." Postmodern man seeks greater understanding. If he is abandoning faith, it is often because the traditional mode of representing religion does not aid understanding in our "jet-nuclear-space" age. Thus faith no longer seems relevant to many people, even to those raised within a religious subculture. In fact, according to recent world trends, greater numbers of people are increasingly seeking not the consolations of the "afterlife" but the comforts of the "good life."

Contemporary youth in the United States, though cool to the appeals of an acquisitive society, prides itself on being a "now generation." Many youth live under a very low ceiling of future expectations with no immediate prospects of raising it. As a result they identify with the films of directors such as Jean-Luc Godard, John Schlesinger, and Richard Lester because their characters have no future, only a present. Whether the adult world likes it or not, youth tends to ignore all parental, scholastic, and religious influences that bypass their present passionate concerns for Vietnam, racial integration, the democratization of educational and economic opportunity, a greater participation in the direction of society and politics, more latitude in forms of life style (hair, dress, and even drugs), and an acceptance of youth as sexually endowed beings. No one will deny that motion pictures face these issues— *now*. Consequently, film has become an outlet for transcendental concerns that are rooted in the human spirit: conscience, guilt, freedom, and love.

In the 1950s the screen became for youth all over the world a type of mecca for a new crusading faith with James Dean as its prophet. Of Dean, Pauline Kael has said: "He is inside the skin of moviegoing and television-watching youth—even educated youth—in a way that Keats and Shelley or John Cornford and Julian Bell are not." One might add with little fear of contradiction that James Dean is inside the skin of youth in a way that Paul Tillich, Karl Rahner, Martin Buber, and other great theologians are not. Our best religious thinkers are not, as Marshall McLuhan put it, "surfboarding along on the electronic wave." Rather, to many people, they give the sense of delivering heady Kierkegaardian wine in musty Cartesian bottles. This is unfortunate because I think that both motion pictures and theology work with transcendence, with the difference that the latter is an elite enterprise and the former oriented to the masses. While seeking recreation, diversion, and understanding, moviewatchers are often exercising transcendental faculties of insight, criticism, and wonder that come remarkably close to what religion has traditionally termed faith, prophecy, and reverence. A wedding of the two is overdue, although, happily, the matchmakers are growing in number.

The moving image is relevant in the contemporary world as little else is. In his *The Age of Discontinuity*, Peter Drucker calls the greatest of discontinuities "the changed position and power of knowledge." Images, as mass movers of knowledge and illusion, can aggravate this discontinuity. They can no longer, therefore, be ignored, especially as a significant mode of religious awareness, though they are obviously different from traditional prayer, liturgy, and acts of piety. Those who profess to be dedicated to religious education and theology should acknowledge the universality of the motion picture experience as one of the foundation stones of an emerging world culture. In default of recognizing an opportunity to use this "imaging" tool for shaping a worldwide religious ethos, it is quite possible that in an "image" civilization of planetary scope, postmodern man may be the hero of a new version of the Book of Job, but a version with no God.

I am indebted to many friends and colleagues for stimulating the ideas presented in this book. Special gratitude is due William Lynch for his past encouragement to develop the ideas presented here and for the inspiration contained in his works on the theological imagination, *The Image Industries* and *Christ and Apollo.* I wish to thank the noted Italian film critic, Nazareno Taddei, who shared with me his views on and personal experiences with such Latin directors as Fellini, Pasolini, Antonioni, and Buñuel. Thanks are also due to Miss Barbara Malley of the Jesuit Writers' Service and to Clayton Carlson, religion editor of Harper & Row, for a number of helpful suggestions regarding the format of the book. Lastly, I wish to express my sincere thanks to my secretary, Mrs. Renée Navarro, for proofreading and typing the manuscript.

NEIL P. HURLEY

Santiago, Chile

Introduction

ROBERT ROSSEN'S *Alexander the Great* presents a vivid account of the Macedonian conqueror's attempt to spread a concept of a world state based on the Greek language, shared customs, and on a mixture of the races of Europe, Africa, and Asia. A disciple of Aristotle, Alexander saw military expansion as a great cross-fertilizing process in which diverse peoples would share the same mind. This concept, called *homonoia*, anticipated in a way Pierre Teilhard de Chardin's ideas about the noosphere by over two thousand years. *Homonoia* was the chief motive for Alexander having thousands of his soldiers take Asian wives, an event stirringly portrayed in Rossen's filming of the great mass marriage ceremony at Susa in Persia. What Alexander the Great tried to do by the sword is being accomplished today in less violent but more effective ways by electronic media.

Largely through the influence of media, we are witnessing what William Ernest Hocking referred to as the emergence of "civilization in the singular." The discovery of the electromagnetic spectrum means that all peoples will be exposed to a single "attention frame," largely by means of the same visual experiences. The idea is fraught, on the one hand, with splendor, namely of a planet in peaceful communion and, on the other, with terror, that is to say of world powers competing to dominate the global village. In either event, the historical course of events which leads to *homonoia* seems irreversible. The dream of Alexander the Great will be realized, even if in the form of a futuristic nightmare.

In Stanley Kubrick's *2001: A Space Odyssey*, reference is made to the concept of *homonoia*. The final scene shows the human embryo as a symbol for nascent cosmic awareness within the membrane of the world's womb. There the moving image plays a critical role through the graphics generated on the computer console screen and the live picture-phone conversation and the television screen bringing satellite-relayed programs from earth. *2001* seems an accurate projection of mankind's future when the image will link human feeling, thought, and behavior on this planet. The critical question is: What will be the quality of communications in a world where every part of the globe can be in instantaneous "sight-sound" contact with every other place on earth? Race, culture, sex, age, social class, and religion have been the subgeneric barriers to universal understanding and tolerance. These barriers do not cause us to *have*

Courtesy: United Artists Corporation.

Richard Burton in *Alexander the Great*.

prejudices so much as to *be* prejudices. Will, then, the moving image indulge these prejudices, confirm them, be indifferent to them, or unmask them? Is there a way the image can serve that reason which, after all, is the universal spark of the divine which the Stoic philosophers believed to bind all men together in some mysterious cosmic fraternity? On the eve of a species-wide system of ocean-spanning wireless signals, is there a transcendent message that can vault the subgeneric barriers just mentioned?

Those tempted to answer negatively offer solid arguments that we in the United States have not improved mass taste over time. Members of cultural and religious elites feel that mass media inescapably levels downward. Since commercial media will continue to exercise great influence in this century, the argument continues that we cannot hope for any mosaic world civilization where respect for subgeneric differences can be neatly harmonized into a larger meaningful whole. This book rests on other assumptions. For fifty years motion pictures, undoubtedly a major contributory force to our new planetary civilization, have succeeded repeatedly in riveting the attention of audiences across every conceivable boundary on themes of universal import. They have uplifted these same audiences as well. Proof of this was given very early in the industry's history by Charlie Chaplin's lovable tramp, known by such names as Charlot, Carlos, Carlitos, and Kärlchen. Chaplin not only entertained but he also inspired the common man to see himself in the anonymous circumstances of urban society as a David fighting the Goliath of society. The adherents of different cultures, races, classes, generations, and sex laughed heartily at Chaplin as he touched our universal chord of empathy.

It is particularly urgent for religious educators and theologians to begin thinking about a similar species-wide message at the outset of satellite communications. Certainly some transcredal belief system will emerge by the year 2000. Behavioral scientists tell us that changes in the technical and social structure bring concomitant changes in the symbolic structure. Accordingly, worldwide communications will shape some planetary consensus regarding transcendental values such as freedom, conscience, guilt, death, and redemptive love, subjects found treated in every culture, every religion, and every period of history, even if under distinctive images.

Who will deny Hocking's statement that the day of private and local religion is over, that we are witnessing the demise of parochialism together with the plurality of civilization? What, then, we may ask, will take its place? Is there any historical form of religion that has not had its mission and message conditioned and thus rendered arbitrarily discriminating by both the "world-image" and "self-image" of the "chosen" trustees? Is there no hope of some master, not necessarily controlling, "religious image" that can have universal appeal to the citizens of our global village?

Hocking offers some hope that there is. He feels that our entire world space is being permeated more and more with ideas, religious and profane, that belong to man as man and not as a member of a society, a culture, a subculture, a profession or an institution. Basically, Hocking believes that in our present postmodern world there has been a greater rapprochement between East and West in terms of identifying certain "unlosables," those durable, persistent residuals of technique and insight that outlast the rise and fall of civilization.

The problem is that Christianity, with its claim to inherent universality, has been resisted much more than the techniques that it has helped unwittingly to produce by shaping the period of modernity from Descartes to Heidegger, with its accent on the scientific method. Western Christianity has fathered a secular attitude that has produced the arts of unlimited human communications without shaping its mission and message to meet the intuitive demands of a world exposed to sight, sound, and data communications in ever growing quantity. The same challenge of using the new media for diffusing its religious patrimony also exists for the non-Christian religions as well. The worldwide cinema culture can help theologians pose relevant questions regarding the transcendental elements of all creeds.

The social historian Arnold Hauser talks of how the moviegoer "experiences the greatness of his cities, the miracles of his technics, the wealth of his ideas, the hidden depths of his psychology in the contiguity, the interconnections and dovetailing of things and processes."[1] In other words, the technique of moviemaking has helped give rise to a mass form of art and entertainment in which psychology is as important as logic, where emotion plays more of a role than reason, and where mood and feeling outweigh moral precepts and religious commandments. If Hauser is correct, then the "imaging revolution" ushered in by the silent film has become for the world public a universal, not merely of technique but of insight. Shortly after World War I came the end of what Marshall McLuhan has called the era of "typographic man."[2] For it was about that time that a global audience could for a modest sum see the classic works of an American (D. W. Griffiths), an Englishman (Charlie Chaplin), a German (G. W. Pabst), an Italian (Enrico Guazzoni), a Swede (Victor Sjostrom), a Dane (Mauritz Stiller), and a Russian (Sergei Eisenstein).[3] Motion pictures exercised in those days a magnetism that we fail to appreciate in our day of more select films and less frequent moviegoing. Women vibrated in empathy with Greta Garbo in her tragic portrayals of Anna Karenina, Queen Christina, and Mata Hari. Man learned about *femmes fatales* such as Pola Negri and Marlene Dietrich and identified with heroes such us William S. Hart, Douglas Fairbanks, and Ramón Novarro. Later in the sound era children were to learn about the Wild West, gangsterism, war, and the adult world by watching James Cagney, Jean Gabin, Fredric March, Marlon Brando, and Paul Newman.

Unfortunately, because motion pictures have been seen largely as a profit-seeking venture, educators, parents, and cultural guardians of society have been late to recognize their potential to form and inform, thus creating the bases of community, through shared experiences at the affective and cognitive levels. One reason is that the image is so close to us that we take it for granted. Curiously, children understand pictures more readily than adults as Antoine de Saint-Exupéry indicated in *The Little Prince*.[4] Whenever he drew a boa constrictor that had swallowed an elephant, adults thought it was a hat until he drew the elephant inside the swollen body of the boa constrictor. Something very similar takes place in the cinema. We see the thematic expression but not the nonthematic reality with which the film artists have to work. The hidden elephant in every media experience is the set of rules of the particular communications game.

For instance, there are six such rules that explain why motion pictures are capable of creating intercultural and interfaith bonds among peoples of the world:

1. A physical law: a transparent plastic material sufficiently flexible to unwind from a reel can produce a number of swiftly moving still images.

2. A physiological law: an image on the retina of the eye persists long enough to give the illusion of continuity when successive still pictures are passed rapidly before a spectator.

3. A psychological law: through skillful editing and montage, induced associations from memory, mind, and imagination can suggest the inner life of persons photographed in illusory motion.

4. A sociological law: any group of individuals emerges more cohesive in sentiment and purpose after a common experience in communication.

5. An anthropological law: people have curiosity about other people and want to learn how they meet the four essential whats of life: a) survival and development, b) love and hate, c) authority and disobedience, and d) ideological systems, i.e., integration in the present social order or protest against it.

6. A religious principle: people will identify negatively with forms of evil and villainy and positively with sacrifice, suffering, and selfless forms of love.*

It is interesting that these six rules of cinematic experience seem to be bound up inextricably with certain constants of reality. In effect, man has discovered a way of recording through sight and sound experiences of nature, life, and human activity so that a mirror image of reality permits man to discover himself and the world about him in greater depth. If one accepts the six rules of the motion picture medium as stated above, then he will be in a position to understand my tempered optimism on the possibility of a trans-credal belief system through globe-encompassing images.

The interplay of all these technological, behavioral, artistic, and spiritual principles were well understood by the late Robert Flaherty, who searched among primitive peoples for those transcendental movements of the human spirit that we "civilized" people often

*This idea was originally developed in my article, "Using Motion Pictures to Aid Inter-Cultural Communication," *The Journal of Communication*, Vol. 18, No. 2 (July 1968).

miss due to our conventional way of seeing life. As Frances Flaherty has pointed out, her husband's contribution to the motion picture was a method of discovery called nonpreconception, "a sort of abandonment, a letting-go, a surrender of the self to that which is greater than the self, beyond the self, so that which is greater and beyond may be brought to light."[5] It is this same principle of discovery, this same disciplined habit following reality to speak for itself, which we believe can help mankind to work at identifying a religious ethos as universal as our communications potential.

This philosophy of nonpreconception, if applied to the world treasury of films, can yield some astonishing insights regarding man's ethico-religious development. It was C. S. Lewis's contention in *The Abolition of Man* that "seeing through something is to see something through it."[6] What do we see, if anything, beneath the diversity of forms of human behavior? Film critics, motion picture reviewers, and movie directors have offered us time and again their view of the world, often even on moral, religious, and theological subjects. Even such a skeptic and debunker as Luis Buñuel in his most iconoclastic films (e.g., *Le Chien Andalou* and *L'Age d'Or*) is trying to help the audience to see something, not merely through something. It is not enough to clear away the tropical overgrowth of superstition, emotion, and taboos; one must also explain why they form part of the human condition. The destruction of one illusion only prepares the way for the next.

In Michelangelo Antonioni's *Blow-Up*, the testimony of the professional photographer is presented as meaningless without the supporting photographic evidence of a murder in the park. Antonioni is posing the problem of the valid criteria of truth: Is reality what we agree upon or is there a purely objective norm? The question is at least as old as Plato's discussion of the prisoners in the cave in Book Seven of *The Republic*. In contrast to Antonioni in *Blow-Up*, Plato not only doubts reality but questions it; he does not merely see through the veils of social reality but sees beneath them to something deeper. His dialogic method shifts the assumptions from ridiculous to sublime and back again until the mind rests where it wishes. Similarly, Flaherty in his films contrasted our civilized assumptions and those of preindustrial cultures. Such a contrast can be enriching as Kenneth Boulding indicated in his book, *The Image*, since it illuminates "the way in which the total image grows, determines or at least limits the directions of future growth."[7] Hopefully, through such a contrasting approach of non-preconception can be discovered the dim outlines of a cinematic theology, whose insights may disclose themselves as persuasive because all cultures, all major world religions, and all races have tenaciously held on to them in one form or another throughout the ages.

This study presupposes religious transcendence in some form as a constant of man, society, and culture. Transcendence is not a static quality in man but the dynamic piston in man's movement toward truth, enabling him to know and even later to sharpen his focus of what he knew mistily, at times falsely. It is precisely this restless onward dynamism which is the heart of human cognition and love and thus of the religious act. Let us take the example of the critic, the iconoclast, the debunker. Whoever sees through something, even through religious hypocrisy, puritanism and pharasaic "legalism," is exercising transcendence and, essentially, is borrowing critical light from the same source as organized religions and, we might add, as atheists and agnostics. For this reason, the author agrees with those who see in Luis Buñuel's films a tortured, traumatic form of what is indubitably an intense religious commitment. This anomaly can only be explained by some dynamic transcendental impulse in all men. It is, then, this assumption which gives us hope for a genuine transcredal belief-system free of partisanship and polemics.

The alliance of cinema and theology that this volume suggests could give mankind the compass it needs as our spaceship earth steers a precarious course between technics and thought. A cinematic theology could assist mankind in anticipating what is around the next historical corner, as we shall see in a later chapter on the futuristic scenarios adumbrated by motion picture artists. These scenarios are secular prophecy, if taken in the aggregate. Theologians would do well to study them as clues to the quality of Hocking's "civilization in the singular."

How can a cinematic theology successfully join religious prophecy with artistic inspiration? One interesting example is Mark Robson's *Nine Hours to Rama*, in which J. S. Casshyap played the role of the Indian leader, Mahatma Gandhi. The climax of the film is the assassination. Vincent Sheean, the distinguished foreign correspondent, reported on the occasion of the film's premiere that Gandhi had a premonition of his death. He felt that the prolongation of his life by modern drugs and medical science proved nothing, adding: "It may be that it is better for me to die."[8] What was significant about this death was not solely the sorrow of his departure but its redemptive quality. As he told Vincent Sheean, "Nobody listens to me any more. If they did, they would not be killing each other."[9] He sensed that in death perhaps the antagonism between the Hindus and Pakistanis might abate. As it turned out, his assassination transcended partisan interests. By touching a universal human chord, it united people by catapulting them beyond their narrow ego-related concerns. As Sheean said: "The true significance of his death is not individual at all, but in the effect, concentrically progressing, of a single event upon all mankind."[10] The ancient Greeks knew the power of catharsis and held drama festivals with religious themes that were open to all citizens, rich and poor alike. *Nine Hours to Rama*, like the tragedies of Aeschylus, Sophocles, and Euripides, also purges us of pity and fear.

Will our "civilization in the singular" be united by the sentiments produced by great tragedy such as the violent death of the gentle Gandhi? Or will it be united in less human, less spiritual ways—by terror, by propaganda, by intrigue? We will know the answer by the end of this decade as the moving image becomes wedded to orbiting artificial satellites to become the constitutive, the representative, and the decisive social experience of the human race. Not forgetting that motion pictures are a major staple of television fare, let us analyze the mounting importance of the movie image for a budding world society.*

First of all, motion pictures will be constitutive in the global village to the extent that pictures will occupy large segments of time in man's day. Leaving aside the "image" communications of tomorrow's world of picture phones and wall television screens, we find that in 1970 some 25 billion people will have watched films shown on movie projectors, that is, six times the number of the world

*This analysis was first developed in my article, "Picture of the Future," *America* (February 13, 1965).

population. To this should be added the sustained "image" experiences of some billion people with access to an estimated 300 million television sets in the world. We should recall that in less industrialized urban and rural areas it is common for ten to twenty people or more to gather around a community receiver. This is why *Life*, in a special double issue dedicated to the cinema, said that motion pictures "are the universal language, the great global educator."[11] Film will provide the bulk of those "image" experiences that are for a great many the third most important activity after work and sleep.

Secondly, motion pictures will be decisive because they will determine to a great extent the self-image of individuals and groups. Just as the image of a Mahatma Gandhi, a Churchill, a John Kennedy, or a Pope John XXIII occupies a strategic center in the lives of the masses, so too do the images of certain stars—Greta Garbo, Rudolph Valentino, James Dean, Marilyn Monroe, Humphrey Bogart. Not only do these legendary images reach hundreds of millions of people eager to emulate someone, they provide an emotional release as well.

We know that the role of mythology in ancient societies was precisely to provide a corpus of images that would serve as a kind of library of scripts for the individual personality as it develops.[12] All young people suffer through the seething internal drama of becoming one of multiple latent identities among whom the ego must choose. Motion pictures are the commonly shared experiences whereby youth especially seek to be mythologically instructed so it may attribute some meaning to a flow of otherwise amorphous inner impulses struggling for public expression. Our religious educators and theologians would do well to study just how universally decisive in the lives of young people are films such as *Rebel Without a Cause*, *Midnight Cowboy*, *Breathless*, *Easy Rider*, *Medium Cool* and *Woodstock*. These films provide the grammar of myth, invariably a necessity for those for whom the grammar of experience is acquired much more slowly.

Lastly, motion pictures will be among the representative social experiences of the species by shaping the way both individuals and communities view the world of the "unseen environment." The televised image and the film image, often interchangeable, will grow to become increasingly the mirror in which modern man looks to gather understanding of the complexity of life in the space age. The hunger for information and vicarious experience will not abate; on the contrary, it will amount steadily in the coming decade. Particularly the "know-not" groups (the illiterates, the unskilled, the poor, and the pre-teenagers) are certain to learn more about the complexities of our emerging world civilization through the image than through literature about ethics, philosophy, religion, and theology. The camera's image will be the most timely, popular, and effective way for people to learn about the shrinking planet. Through the camera will come the mirror images of the outer world, causing motion pictures to be among the representative experiences of our rapidly emerging "civilization in the singular."

Having established the basic procedure of this study, I wish to stress its exploratory nature. It is a primer, not a rigorously logical system of doctrine such as one finds in the classic works of theology. Given its cinematic character and its interest in transcredal

Courtesy: Warner Bros., Inc.

James Dean in *Rebel Without a Cause.*

types of theological affirmations, it could not purport to be anything more. My one objective is to impress on theologians, educators, and representatives of the major world religions that for tens of millions of people the motion picture experience enjoys a psychological and pedagogical legitimacy that has as yet not been matched by a corresponding effectiveness in the modes of religious communication. The application of Marshall McLuhan's famous dictum, "The medium is the message," is nowhere more illuminating and more disturbing than in the field of religion, in which for generations, even centuries, textual communications and their memorization have played a great role. Access to an "imaging" medium such as motion pictures offers educators, theologians, and religious leaders an exhilarating opportunity to compare their messages with those expounded by others. For the truly religious man desirous of giving witness to a revelation and not a propagandistic ideology, films can be providential.

Three points remain to be clarified before analyzing a cinematic theology as the basis for a religious ethos of species-wide acceptability. The first point is that we are neither proposing nor promoting a religious eclecticism, some form of religious Esperanto which, having been designed for all uses and tastes, ends by not satisfying the religious aspirations of any group whatsoever. We know that the Romans filled their Pantheon with gods from all the provinces and territories over which they reigned without seeing any contradiction or feeling any disloyalty to their own gods and goddesses. All gods were equal, because no God made any singular claims to be worshiped uniquely. The weakness of democracy is to level downward. Our intention, perhaps impossibly utopian, is to level upward. The effort toward such a goal must be made in any event.

The second point to be made concerns the author's own preconceptions, if that is the word. As a Christian, the author enjoys his own image of how religion will face the coming "civilization in the singular." For instance, he feels with Hocking that the freedom of individuals to define their own ultimate loyalties "is beyond any institutional authority's competence," thus allowing people on their earthly pilgrimage to assess their transcendental commitments according as they judge the evidence of the life-process. Furthermore, the author concurs that as Christianity is relieved progressively of its peculiar forms of "westernism," it will reveal itself in inspiring simplicity as having the same truly universal visible essence it has preached to the world through almost twenty centuries. Having said this, the reader will probably share the conviction of the author that Christianity will be heavily taxed in this century to prove that it is as universal as the religious points of consensus presented in this study. It is the author's personal belief that Christianity will meet this test, even if only with painful struggle.

Thirdly, the merit of such a study as this is that all religions must test their claims to universality by the potential reach of media such as motion pictures. Such media serve as a discipline on one's faith, not an obstacle. A cinematic theology, far from displacing existing religions, can help them, even force them, to rid the ship of religion, whatever colors it may be flying, from those barnacles which prevent it from reaching port faster. In this regard, the reader will certainly have his own criteria for identifying the barnacles. Important in this matter is not to have truth on our side but rather facts, reasons and persuasive arguments. Only if we are willing to expand our truth-field to crowd out untruths, can we come to the light, the light of transcendence and beyond to a deeper communion with God and other men. The optimism of this study lies in the assumption that man, as spirit, is open to truth, if he will but fairly test reality.

1

Religious Man in Secular Society

HERBERT MARCUSE has noted that the "traditional borderlines between psychology on the one side and political and social philosophy on the other have been made obsolete by the condition of man in the present era."[1] Marcuse maintains that, as long as privacy was real and self-determined, the individual could pursue a destiny independently of social forces. Today, with the increase of secularization, the conditions of both psychological freedom and religious commitment are inescapably linked to urban technological forces. The movie *Lilies of the Field* vividly illustrates the conditions of freedom and religious commitment in a secular context. Homer Smith (Sidney Poitier) is a latter-day nomad who can strategically drop in and out of society as he sees fit. Hence he preserves his autonomy from the growing social and institutional forces, both profane and religious, that exert such a pull of gravity on man's transcendence.

Homer is a self-made man, evidently the product of an urban upbringing with its many pluralistic contacts. Highly inner-directed, he is a peculiar amalgam of self-sufficiency and willingness to serve. He is clearly seen not to be an island, self-satisfied and aloof, but a part of the human continent. He truly cares for others. What is striking is his universal appeal: his willingness to help others, his dignity and self-assuredness and respectful aloofness from confessional practices. One asks: Is Homer a civic saint or a pagan gentleman? Whatever the answer, he seems to be a new model of transcendence within the boundaries described by Harvey

Cox in *The Secular City:* "Contemporary man has become the cosmopolitan. The world has become his city and his city has reached out to include the world. The name for the process by which this has come about is secularization."[2]

First of all, Homer stands out in marked contrast with the refugee East German Catholic sisters upon whom he chances during his travels through the southwestern United States. They are decidedly tradition-directed, taking their cues from their inherited ritual and religious rule. Homer, by comparison, has a fluid "ego system," pragmatic and quick to adapt to changing circumstances. He can carpenter, carry the hod, lay bricks, and drive a bulldozer. His version of truth is decidedly action-oriented, not purely verbal. He "does the truth," as St. Paul said. Because the Mother Superior has a set of predefined expectations of how people should behave, a confrontation between the two types is inevitable.

What draws the reflective viewer's attention in the heated exchange between the refugee nun and the indignant Negro is the persuasive force of the latter. Never before, it would seem, has anyone challenged the religious assumptions of this woman, this strong Mother Superior, who always took for granted the form and substance of her received beliefs. A definite conversion process ensues, in terms not of a turning away from the contents of her faith but rather of insight into its implications in everyday life. Homer becomes, in a peculiar sense, the evangelizing force in the life of these sisters. He deepens their humanity and in so doing brings them closer to their divine calling.

Another noteworthy contrast is between Homer and the Mexican-Americans who appear in the film. Devout but not too practical, they find Homer appealing, for he—like them—loves life. He sings and dances with them, sharing the simple joys that distinguish the Latin temperament from the more Nordic temperament of the nuns. Nevertheless, Homer also differs radically from them. Endowed with what Emerson described as self-reliance, he creates his own work pressures and forges his own destiny. Not only is he tolerant, he also is not afraid to experiment. He is an agent of change who succeeds without threatening people. The Mexican-Americans are not change-oriented. Their social expectations have been inherited from their fathers and go back generations, even

Sidney Poitier in *Lilies of the Field*.

centuries. We can imagine that Homer rejected whatever social mask his ancestors passed on to the generations that succeeded them. He has created his own social identity, breaking with the fatalism that ruled the lives of his slave forebears. While Homer has left a tradition, he does not seem in search of anything new. He certainly does not strike one as alienated. His life style is complete, harmonizing "this-worldliness" with the religious sentiments of compassion, service, and sacrifice. He works to help build the chapel for the sisters; he shops for them in the supermarket; he teaches them new songs; he drives them to church. In all this he never feels himself superior in any way. He assumes that this attention is part of being a full human being.

How different his secularism from that of the Mexican-American who has abandoned the "faith of his fathers" to pursue his storekeeper's activities. He has left home culturally as has Homer, but with a difference. He has not found transcendence in the form of service or dignity or sacrifice. He "sees through" the pious veils of faith of his churchgoing compatriots, but unlike Homer, he has not worked out a personal creed or ethic. He is the type of man who, knowing that he is not the only one wrong, rests satisfied with that consoling reminder. If both Homer and the Mexican-American café owner are caught between cultures, at least the former has not settled for conformity to the core values of an acquisitive society as the latter seems to have done. Rather, Homer seems to have made the effort to develop his latent spiritual energies as best he can in new, inventive ways.

The measure of Homer's religiosity is best judged in the scene with the white Anglo-Saxon Southerner whose fundamentalist beliefs prevent him from according full human stature to a Negro. Homer's ability to drive a bulldozer is a sign of initiative that dumfounds the bigot. Interestingly enough, both are Protestants— if not in practice, then in spirit. Homer bristles with all the original indignation that inspired the Protestant movement to set itself against whatever diminished man's freedom to express transcendence as he saw it. The Southerner, on the other hand, is a white Anglo-Saxon fundamentalist within Protestantism and a racist in the bargain. As earlier with the Catholic Mother Superior, here again, Homer's response takes the form of righteous indignation against smugness and dogmatism. Both the Southern WASP and the Catholic nun are kindred spirits, "True believers" in the sense described by Eric Hoffer, namely, those who never doubt because they never question the tacit assumptions of their creed. They lack the "open mind" that Robert Oppenheimer described as that quality which does justice to the implicit, the imponderable and the unknown, which embodies the deference that action pays to uncertainty, and which binds power to reason.[3]

What do we learn of theological significance from *Lilies of the Field?* If nothing else, the lesson that the religious habit does not make either the monk or the man. The reality principle as it is embodied in complex, advanced technological societies does not stop at the threshold of the cloister, the monastery, or the religious sanctuary. Members of long-standing religious institutions and traditions such as the German sisters and the Mexican-American Catholics are no longer free of worldly temptations and delusions as they once were. They must renew their faith constantly in terms of the social and technical changes that happen around them. On the other hand, an apparently areligious person such as Homer reveals traits that evacuate the classical meaning of such terms as atheist, pagan, or rationalist. In Homer we discern a cosmic sense of commitment, which is as constant as it is universal. He is what Scripture calls "a man without guile," a man free of duplicity, one of whom Hamlet has said: "Give me that man that is not passion's slave, and I will wear him in my heart's core, ay, in my heart of heart."

The disquieting feature of today's religious scene is what some have referred to as the "anonymous believer," whose only badge of credence is his personal testimony. If we learn to desist from judging merely according to the received notions of church affiliation and similar external tests, then a film such as *Lilies of the Field* can teach us more existential norms of performance, sincerity, and integrity. With these new standards some surprising discoveries can then be made.

In *A Taste of Honey*, for example, we have a clear instance of the "anonymous apostle." Director Tony Richardson presents a lower class English girl from the Midlands of William Blake's "dark Satanic mills." The daughter of a slatternly mother, Jo is an unwed mother-to-be. As played by Rita Tushingham, Jo at first strikes us as amoral due to her affair with a handsome Negro sailor who leaves to go on a voyage. But, we gradually grow to admire her and sympathize with her, since she bears herself with dignity marked by a lack of self-pity and bitterness. Having known only poverty, disillusionment, and loneliness, we see how environmental pressures thwart her expectations. To quote Gilbert and Sullivan's *The Mikado*, she must play the game of life with "a crooked cue, a cloth untrue and an elliptical billiard ball."

Then comes the bit of "honey" into her life, the homosexual Geoffrey, fascinatingly acted by Murray Melvin. In order to legitimate the child he offers to marry her. Moreover, he dissuades Jo from having an abortion and affectionately prepares for the baby's arrival by seeking information through periodic visits to the maternity clinic. Whatever may have been the pessimism in Shelagh Delaney's original play, Richardson has tempered it with rays of hope. The moralist who sees only ethically deviant patterns of behavior in Jo, her mother Helen, and Geoffrey will miss the pulsating beat of charity, concern, and community that bind marginal social types in ways unfamiliar to those raised in less harsh social and economic circumstances.

A more recent film of John Schlesinger, *Midnight Cowboy*, is another oblique tale of altruism amid misery. A Texas lad (Jon Voigt), comes to New York to begin what he believes will be a dazzling and lucrative career as a "stud" for wealthy, lonely women. He meets "Ratso" Rizzo, a crippled pimp played by Dustin Hoffman. The average moviegoer may be prompted to ask: What can issue from the sewer existence of nighttime Times Square, with its parasitic and pathological denizens? While Schlesinger falls short of creating a film classic, he succeeds in winning us over to the fact that human affection, honest and unpretentious, can flourish even on barren metropolitan sidewalks. The final scene of Rizzo's quiet demise in the arms of his Texan friend on the bus to Miami is not without emotion or theological significance. In some twisted, obscure, antisocial, but nonetheless providential way, we have one more proof of transcendence in the face of seemingly hostile odds.

Mike Nichols's version of Joseph Heller's *Catch 22* documents another reverse lesson concerning human transcendence as it is manifested in a set of pathological pressures generated within an

Air Force group in World War II Europe. The protagonist, Yossarian, is convinced that the commands of his superior officers are based on a peculiar kind of elastic logic that always results in keeping the men from going home despite the number of missions they have flown. He finds this malevolent and a jeopardy to his own life as well as to those of his comrades. To deal with the injustice of the situation, Yossarian chooses to outthink the system rather than to meet it head on. (He never sees himself as a martyr like Joan of Arc or Thomas More.) Each time the number of raids is raised as a condition for being sent home, Yossarian studies how he can find some legal loophole for escaping further duty. "Catch 22" refers to the clause in the military codebook which states that whoever convincingly and logically proves he is mentally unfit for combat *ipso facto* has established his sanity, thus qualifying him to continue as a combatant. A satirical caricature of military life, *Catch 22* makes an important contribution to a theology of man in society, namely, that an abnormal environment distorts the ability of those within it to perceive what is reasonable, what is truthful, what it is that brings man closer to the divine and so to himself.

A similar situation in civilian life is depicted in Dino Risi's *Il Sorpasso*. Not too often does a film succeed in winning the sympathy of the audience at the same time it unmasks them. Chaplin often held up the mirror of caricature to his audience without their realizing that they were laughing at themselves and not at the stock figures who imposed their boorish, bourgeois mores on Charlie, the tramp. So too in this film, Vittorio Gassman plays the typical middle class man of contemporary urban, technological society, intent on getting ahead, achieving, and being accepted. Actually, the character played by Gassman is a failure, a fact he tries to disguise by means of his small white convertible, which allows him to pass the automobiles of those considerably more successful than he. The height of his elation comes when, in passing such people, he can manifest his superiority by honking his horn with its distinctive melody. (Incidentally, "Il Sorpasso" is the Italian expression for a reckless driver.)

The loneliness of Gassman's "Il Sorpasso" brings him to invite a law student on a trip. The student begins to realize that his life has been one of vicarious experience derived from books. He senses the urgency to "live" and so accompanies Gassman. This proves a fatal decision, however. He, who could have served society so well, is killed in a car crash while "Il Sorpasso" survives to play out the charade of life.

We see that in a real sense society becomes interiorized in man insofar as it insinuates its values into him. Is there any escape in societies progressively more secular, more interdependent, more demanding on the human spirit? Can man in secular society be religious anymore? Only if he finds outside of society itself some source of inspiration to support a system of personal transcendence. This is not easy. In fact, the number of persons who succeed may be quite limited since the dark veils that postmodern society inadvertently erects between transcendence and its fulfillment seem to be multiplying. Films such as *Midnight Cowboy*, *A Taste of Honey*, *Catch 22*, and *Il Sorpasso* testify to the growing confusion that complex social structures produce in an increasing number of people. To document this more fully, one could add other such films as *The 400 Blows*, *Shoeshine*, *The Grapes of Wrath*, *Paths of Glory*, *Patterns*, and *Easy Rider*. These films show how radically different our lives are today from the simpler existence of preindustrial societies. Nevertheless, beneath the diverse social forms beats the pulse of religious transcendence.

Courtesy: Janus Films, Inc.

Jean-Pierre Leaud in *400 Blows*.

We have seen how this transcendental reach functions in twentieth-century societies. What, however, of older, less complicated
cultures? Robert Flaherty has been the greatest film exponent to
date on the forms of transcendence in mores and beliefs of precivilized peoples. In *The Liveliest Art*, Arthur Knight describes the
Flaherty sense of nonpreconception that he had learned from the
Eskimos during his shooting of *Nanook of the North*.[4] Flaherty,
distrustful of shooting scripts and prepared plots, went to the South
Seas to film *Moana*. There he discovered that the Samoans were
attuned to nature, not in conflict with it as in societies influenced
by the Greco-Roman tradition of the West. The Samoan gods were
kind; food was abundant through activities such as coconut-gather-
ing, fishing, and bear-hunting; the women made simple garments
and prepared the food; the men constructed the huts and village
centers for feasts, ceremonies, and dances. The Samoan youths had
to undergo a tattoo ritual in order to be certified by the tribe as
full-fledged adults. As long as the white traders did not introduce
new, "civilized" customs, the spirit of competition was absent.

That transcendence takes more the form of serenity—we might
call it passivity—in older agrarian cultures is also seen in Kaneto
Shindo's film, *The Island*. A Japanese family is portrayed, living on
an island without fresh water. Just as in *Men of Aran* Flaherty gave
us a documentary of a community struggling to survive on a barren
isle off the western coast of Ireland, so Shindo has captured the
inexhaustible patience of a family that sees nature as a frugal, if not
downright hostile, landlord. Their principal occupation is ferrying
water back from the mainland and carrying it in buckets on a
shoulder-yoke up a hilly ascent to irrigate their meager crops. Although released in 1961, the film is in effect a silent film. The chief
symbol of man's transcendence, language, is suppressed in order to
convey the total absorption of the family in basic tasks for survival.

The Apu Trilogy of Satyajit Ray is a lyric chronicle of the growth
of a Hindu boy from his youth in the provinces through his manhood in Calcutta and his later marriage and fatherhood.[5] The
chaste, tranquil setting of *Pather Panchali* introduces us to the
serene family life of India. That society is the indispensable condition for religious expression is apparent in Apu's closely knit
household, where there is cultivated reverence for age, nature, the

sacred writings, and for the temple rites—that is whenever fierce economic pressures permit. After the cruel deaths of Apu's grand-mother and sister, his father, a lay priest and healer, moves the family to Benares, where subsequently he too dies. Apu's mother works as a cook to support the family. When she dies, Apu abandons his studies for the priesthood. For him, manhood comes at a costly price.

Whereas the protagonists of *Nanook of the North*, *Moana*, *Men of Aran*, and *The Island* are immersed in a nature where the divine manifests itself as food, drink, and favorable climate, the young Apu is shown as dependent on the bounty of nature and more self-conscious. He is the bridge between the tradition-directed in-habitants of neolithic societies and the other-directed persons of the postmodern electronic societies presented in films such as *8½*, *Blow-up*, *Darling*, *Skidoo*, and *Medium Cool*. That is why *The Apu Trilogy* is crucial to our cinematic theology. It would be interesting to contrast the growth in personality and manliness of Apu with, say, Charlie Gordon in Ralph Nelson's film, *Charly*, and his ac-celerated passage from mental retardation to literacy to superior intelligence and back to mental deprivation. This is by no means to imply that preindustrial people are the equivalents of mentally retarded people. I am only suggesting a method of nonpreconcep-tion to stimulate insights about the religious implications of both personal and social development, however gradual or rapid.

A behavioral theology must not overlook the impact of science and technology on the modes of transcendence that humans adopt.[6] Both the young Apu and the retarded Charly can find their own levels of integration into society if left to their respective resourcefulnesses. This is because transcendence is within the reach of all persons, whatever the accidents of their birth, upbringing, or environment. However, both Apu and Charly are the objects of dynamic forces of change. In Charly's case, the change is highly personal, more abrupt, and directly linked to change in character and spiritual outlook, as we shall see later in a more detailed discus-sion of the film. Apu's new life in Calcutta is a reorganization of his life at its deepest level, while Charlie Gordon's newly activated intelligence potential makes him see his world as utilitarian, with some people exploiting others for profit, prestige, or power. Incidentally; the unusual Czechoslovakian film *Tarzan* develops this same theme, contrasting the life of Tarzan before and after his Western education. Daniel Keyes, the author of the novel *Flowers for Algernon*, which provided the film scenario for *Charly*, has Charlie reproach his scientific patrons: "Here in your university, intelligence, education, knowledge, have all become great idols. But I know now there's one thing you've all overlooked: intelligence and education that hasn't been tempered by human affection isn't worth a damn."[7] Some interesting theological implications for further study are suggested in these remarks and in Charlie's belief ". . . that the mind absorbed in and involved in itself as a self-centered end, to the exclusion of human relationships, can only lead to violence and pain."[8]

One last case study is useful to show how cinema can serve as a faithful "recording angel" for a wide variety of patterns of intersection between personal behavior and social background. In Jean Renoir's classic, *The Rules of the Game*, the curtain of inherited manners is drawn back to reveal the behavior of aristocrats during a weekend at a French country estate. Renoir shows us how aristo-

Through the courtesy of Cinema Releasing Corporation.

Cliff Robertson in *Charly*.

cratic values, as a residual of medieval courtly codes of behavior, are being eroded by the acid of modernity. Renoir seems to be saying that chivalric customs, once an organic part of the culture of Christian Europe, can easily become an empty shell, cracked by circumstances and convenience. The unregenerate precivilized instincts are easily awakened and manage to counteract the long-standing social responses to which the figures in Renoir's farce have been conditioned. If time can drain away the energy of original motivation, then the "rules of the game" will be drawn anew around other more meaningful social priorities. Rarely has the lacquer of custom been more neatly peeled away, and rarely has the "downward resourcelessness" of class-conditioned ethics been more adroitly exposed. Buñuel, incidentally, did something similar for lower class values in *Viridiana*, although more sardonically and less artfully.

What can be concluded from this review of films bearing on an environmental theology? Six ideas open to further research have arisen out of this discussion, hypotheses that are open to testing not only in film but in other art forms, and even in life itself.

The first principle is that as human relationships become more intertwined in urban, technological cultures, they tend to be mutually supportive. This highly interdependent set of social factors constitutes a reality principle that blurs the classic distinction bestowed by Western civilization between the clergy and the laity. In *Lilies of the Field*, Homer becomes by any fair test the Christian par excellence. It is he who deepens the faith of the sisters, who helps them to serve the Mexican-American community better, and who serves as a constructive agent of change in the lives of those whom he meets (the Mexican-American café owner, the Catholic priest, and the Southern bigot). The recent stress by American Jewish and Christian communities that social commitment must be an expression of solid religious commitment seems to corroborate the plot dynamics of *Lilies of the Field* and its secular humanist creed.

This leads to a corollary statement also evident in *Lilies of the Field*, namely, that the secularization process, far from being either intrinsically evil or dispassionately neutral, is a necessary social condition in pluralistic societies so that man may gain distance from obstacles to his transcendental reach such us total institutionalization, political, cultural and social ideologies, economic subservience, and religious dogmatism. The Mother Superior, while more benign than her more austere counterpart in *A Nun's Story*, is still authoritarian, wishing subjects and even nonsubjects such as Homer to come out where she wants them to, irrespective of their liberty, conscience, or feelings. Unlike the sisters, Homer can answer back. He is a free agent, with other sources of information, other standards of judgment, other income potentials, and other ways to serve the same God that the Mother Superior worships. Harvey Cox has addressed himself to this open-ended kind of social situation, which for the unprepared can be baffling, but for the initiated such as Homer very liberating.[9]

Having granted a positive valence to secularization by describing Homer as one of its proudest trophies, there logically follows a third postulate for an environmental theology: the concept of the "anonymous believer." This refers to the nonaffiliated person who fulfills high ethical and spiritual norms without being conscious of it in the way that a religious person is. Homer's case is an obvious one. He is unpretentious, spontaneous, and totally transparent. He seems to be better at his creed than all the traditional Christians portrayed in the film are at theirs.

The more difficult applications of this postulate come where kindness, compassion, and goodness are mingled in generous quantities with persons who are considered "deviants" by society. In *A Taste of Honey* an exquisite form of charity is shown. Similarly in *Midnight Cowboy*, the Texas male prostitute is genuinely concerned about the health of his tubercular friend and manager. *Catch 22*, with its battle-weary, neurotic, and opportunistic hero, offers us an eccentric, but real manifestation of transcendence in terms of a search for justice, liberty, and peace. Cinema has often documented, frequently in impressively artistic ways, those truncated saints who heroically remain faithful to transcendental impulses in bizarre ways. What a cinematic theology can do is to show how often our middle class ethics misjudge persons whose net assets in terms of character, charity, and charisma outweigh their liabilities. At times, the traditional prescriptions regarding morality, propriety, and doctrine are transformed because the social and technical factors in the process of change are not anticipated and prepared for. Environment, physical or psychic, changes man's values. This fact, reflected in cinema, makes imperative a search for the positive elements in the transitional patterns of religious belief and practice that are unfolding before us. The "anonymous believer" like Homer is obviously drawing motivation from some transcendental source that even he cannot explain, a source that is open to all people, not exclusively to those who were rocked in their cradles with religious lullabies and taught simple night prayers as part of "the faith of our fathers."

The fourth axiom in drafting an environmental theology could well be the "anonymous creed" unconsciously but effectively exuded by a society, culture, or civilization. There are obvious examples of explicitly ideological social systems, such as Nazi Germany, Fascist Italy, and Communist Russia. In these three cases there were definite ethical and theological assumptions underlying the superstructure of political and military convictions. To this degree we can speak of an "anonymous creed" emanating from a milieu. In *Il Sorpasso*, the role played by Vittorio Gassman was conditioned by the acquisitive society in which he lived. His car with its horn, its speed, and its color bestowed on him a sense of adequacy, indeed, even superiority, thus hiding from him—but not from the perceptive viewer—the shallowness of his life with its yearning for status, conspicuous consumption, and security. These values can easily be interiorized when culture envelops its members as thoroughly as our urban, technological societies do.

The fifth principle is that precivilized societies dispose their members to satisfy transcendental needs in different ways than contemporary postmodern societies bent on technological advance, competition, capital accumulation, and consumption. The works of Robert Flaherty present proof of the subordinate role economics played in serving cultural ends. *Moana*, for instance, shows the Samoan people's harmony with nature, how they submerged their economic activities in social and family relationships. Ritual worship and communal tasks were all related to economic survival in such cultures. While fatalism and even passivity color the religious outlook of primitive and neolithic peoples, their belief systems—such as nature worship, animism, and pantheism—presumed harmony with and a dependence upon natural forces decidedly different from the assumptions of a consumer society such as that treated in *Il Sorpasso*. *The Apu Trilogy* is an excellent link in explaining how man has evolved from the one extreme of barter economics to the other of capital-intensive market economics. Ray has charted well Apu's progressive development from a rural lad to an adult city dweller with a family, and his resulting changes in outlook. Apu is a modern man in contemporary Calcutta but his roots lie in the Hindu tradition of Gandhi's cottage industries.

The sixth principle is concerned with the decay, renewal, and rebirth of societies with an explicit credal commitment, such as the European Christian tradition that ruled the upper classes of France in *The Rules of the Game*. If, indeed, there is an "anonymous creed" latent in all social systems, then we can easily discern that societies resting on a base of revelation or some religious patrimony must constantly rediscover, reassimilate, and reinforce the original inspiration of the community. If not, it progressively weakens and reaches a critical threshold where a socioreligious vacuum is created. Into this vacuum will filter some "anonymous creed," as in *Il Sorpasso*, where an affluent Italy, impaled on Marxist and capitalistic ideologies, can little boast of being the Roman Catholic hegemony it once was. Another example of the erosion of a long-standing religious culture is the unqualified adoption of scientism in the America which serves as the *mise en scéne* for *Charly*.

Renoir's film depicts a crucial point at which the social dynamics of the Catholic church's oldest daughter, France, have transformed the aristocratic practice of Catholicism into the mere luminous glow of a flickering, spent candle. Renoir paints for us the unattractive face of milieu Christianity, to all intents and purposes the social equivalent of the "whited sepulchre" to which Matthew's Gospel refers. What Renoir does humorously in *The Rules of the Game*, Buñuel has done more savagely in *L'Age d'Or* and *Viridiana*, unmasking both the middle class pharisaism and the mystique of poverty. Both directors have shown how society serves as the battleground where two rival creeds meet, one based on a century-old religious tradition socially accepted but no longer ascendant, the other a struggling, still inchoate creed that, though not legitimated or institutionalized effectively, directs the feelings, thoughts, and choices of a growing number of people.

2

Man as Inner Center

THE FILM *If* . . . presents the occupants of a military boarding school in England: the headmaster, his wife, the chaplain, the nurse, the faculty, the student trustees, and the students. Our attention is drawn to three upperclassmen in particular. They seem alert, questioning, and highly independent. They are no longer influenced by the school, an inference founded on the pictures that decorate their dormitory walls: pin-ups of movie beauties, guerrillas, and starving natives. They are obviously under the sway of other educational influences outside the institution. The school that proudly taught their docile fathers and grandfathers now regretfully teaches these rebellious lads. The film is not unlike Renoir's *Rules of the Game* insofar as it portrays a subculture whose vitality has been ebbing gradually. Since the institutional shell is often the last to undergo change, the three boys contemplate revolution.

What must be emphasized in considering the film *If* . . . is the distortion in personality development a fossilized institution can cause. We expect abnormalities, repression, and perversion in corrective institutions such as were shown in *I Was a Fugitive from a Chain Gang, Cool Hand Luke*, and *Riot*. However, in an upper class military school of long-standing tradition, the average person is shocked to imagine how warped so many people have become through the impact of total institutionalization. The film perplexes us somewhat because the boundaries between reality and fantasy are made to swim as in Luis Buñuel's *Belle du Jour* or Alain Resnais' *Last Year at Marienbad*. Consequently, we never know in what order of reality we are. The plot branches off suddenly and without warning, mingling real happenings with "wish-fathered" thoughts presented as though they were actually taking place. If we accept the religious assumptions of writers such as St. Augustine, who maintained that the intent is tantamount to the deed, then the portrayal of wishes and suppressed desires becomes significant. We begin to pierce the masks that social roles represent to see the quality of life of the school's inhabitants: the fetishistic desires of the headmaster's wife, the autism of the nurse, the homosexual tendencies of the trustee, the cruelty of the punishments meted out, the arbitrariness of the school's decision-making process, and finally, the imperious will to revenge by the three boys bent on destroying the system. The final scene, probably imaginary, has its logical antecedents in the merciless caning scene. As a meaningless, vindictive reflex rather than as a reasoned punitive measure, the caning shocks us into accepting the justice of violently putting a stop to a retrograde system whose momentum and direction could easily go on for another decade. Lindsay Anderson, the film's director, leaves us with no doubt as to the feelings of the boys. With them, we wonder not only about the irrelevance and waste of such miseducation but about the personal harm to the development of character as well.

Whether or not we accept the final scene of the rooftop massacre of the guests and participants at the graduation ceremony, the seeds of revolutionary debacle have been sown, and irrevocably so. They will very likely bear fruit in some mysterious way, perhaps on other premises than those of the school. This film, remarkable for its penetration into the contemporary student psyche, confirms a well-known constant of human behavior: the determination of free agents to escape from repressive social structures.

If man exercises his transcendence in social situations, then not only the persons, groups, and institutions around him are affected, but he, too, is modified. The interior core of human personality is not an impregnable fortress protected from the outer world by a moat and drawbridge. It is a social product that an individual can selectively shape through imagination, reflection, and decision. The cinema has explored this psychological world, helping us to understand better the interrelations between self and society. Lindsay

Anderson's *If . . .* depicts how man manages to vault over the constraints of his immediate physical environs in order to satisfy a transcendental need that is denied socially. It is a valuable contribution, for this reason, to a cinematic theology.

This desire for freedom is no respecter of persons. It can be the rebellion of the young against society (*Wild in the Streets*), the rebellion against the military (*The Bofors Gun*), the rebellion against religious authority (*Martin Luther*), the rebellion against political measures (*The Birth of a Nation*), or the rebellion against economic injustice (*On the Waterfront*). The dangers of pent-up psychic forces cannot be underestimated. Hence coercive measures such as capital punishment, indemnities, police action, and threats of reprisals are only partial deterrents. If social situations cannot be made to respond flexibly to the deeper aspirations of people, then history shows that the chemistry of violent change will serve as the catalyst.

Perhaps the finest screen study of psychopathic repression on an individual level is Fritz Lang's *M,* starring Peter Lorre as the Düsseldorf murderer of a small girl. We see the sexually disturbed killer study himself in the mirror, a prisoner of narcissistic impulses. This revelatory scene brings to a sharp focus the workings of an inner reality, the unconscious of M. What shaped this perverted will? What was the social context that served as the matrix from which emerged those urges which, so logical to M, are so illogical to us? If in *If . . .* we were shown the institutional provocation, in *M* no social diagnosis is given. At best, it can only be inferred.

M is important for a behavioral theology because it makes plausible a thesis which the law and psychoanalysis accept but which the average man of common sense is not always ready to believe: crime is not always a personally responsible act. If man is, to a certain extent, society interiorized, then the shadowy underground of social existence can form human beings into its own likeness. It is noteworthy that serious films often give us insights into the protagonist's earlier history: *In Cold Blood, Wild in the Streets, The Goddess, Midnight Cowboy,* and *Citizen Kane.* If the child is father to the man, as Wordsworth held, then we must try to reconstruct the life process that formed the motivating idea of the person involved. In *M,* Fritz Lang has the trapped murderer cry out: "I can't help myself!" Pauline Kael attributes Lorre's superb acting to the fact "that he makes us understand the terrified, suffering human being who murders." Richard Brooks and Arthur Penn have succeeded in awakening the same understanding in *In Cold Blood* and in *Bonnie and Clyde* respectively. As Madame de Stäel once said: "Tout comprendre, c'est tout pardonner!"—To understand is to forgive! Unless there is evidence to the contrary, we should always assume that perpetrators of inhuman deeds must somewhere have been subjected to inhuman pressures.

At least, this is the humanistic, indeed religious, conclusion that closes Akira Kurosawa's film, *High and Low*. The plot features the internationally known star, Toshiro Mifune, as an industrialist who consents to pay the ransom for the return of his chauffer's son, kidnaped by mistake in place of his own son. After a police search the kidnaper is arrested and jailed. Mifune goes to speak to him. Across the plateglass retainer each confronts the other, and we see that social injustice and private misdeeds are woven of the same seamless cloth. The kidnaper, bred in poverty, nurtured a resentment against Mifune's large house on the hill, while the kidnaping brought financial ruin to Mifune. The question of life as the great complicity in which we all share—whether we like it or not—is the lesson of *High and Low*. Instead of the wrongdoer and the wronged, Kurosawa teaches us that responsibility is independent of wealth, poverty, and of arbitrary legal criteria of guilt and innocence. What is socially defined often becomes *ipso facto* a psychological definition. In societies where opportunity, wealth, and position are badly distributed among the populace, the high and the low equally become victims, but in different ways. Kurosawa makes a significant contribution to cinematic theology by forcing our gaze beyond the precarious veils of social conventions to the psychological, the moral, and the eschatological. If guilt is shared willingly, as the end of *High and Low* suggests, then can there be any divine retribution beyond the state's sentence? Few films bring us to the interior foundations of so-called criminal action as this one does. It brings out what Donald Richie has called the central thesis of Kurosawa's work, that "man must fight to retain hope in the midst of this hopeless world and in this fight all men are brothers."[1]

This leads to a further thought: If the human soul cannot help but

Barry Shear's *Wild in the Streets*. A scene from the American International Picture *Wild in the Streets*.

Jacques Tati's *My Uncle*.

bear the psychic imprint of social structures and the expectations they tacitly impose, then somehow the development of human transcendental potentials must be related to social expectations. We have already seen how society nurtures certain values of a crypto-theological nature. How, then, can the majority of persons develop spiritually in a society with a low level of spiritual ideals, such as in *If. . ., Il Sorpasso,* and *The Rules of the Game?* And how can those with traumatic childhoods blossom supernaturally, as in *M, The Goddess, In Cold Blood, Wild in the Streets,* and *Midnight Cowboy?* As the upper side of a tapestry hides the knotted stitches of the underside, so, too, the giant web of social circumstances may conceal the spiritual loose ends that have been clipped and tied carelessly together in the lives of countless individuals.

Rare are the *cinéastes* who have attempted to tabulate the spiritual costs of civilization. Chaplin, Flaherty, Renoir—and even Buñuel in his own surrealistic way—are among the names that suggest themselves. More recently another social critic and humanist has appeared on the scene: Jacques Tati, the French mimic and director. In his celluloid critiques of man at work (*The Big Day*), of man at play (*Mr. Hulot's Holiday*), and of man at home with his family (*My Uncle*), he has fashioned a triptych of sardonic comments on human nature in a civilization based on speed, flight from ennui, and the search for comfort. Beside this, he parallels scenes of an older, slower way of life, nostalgic frames of country fairgrounds, mail deliveries by bicycle, old town squares, village taverns, friendly quarrels over back fences, fishmongers, mongrel dogs, street arabs, sunlight and canaries, grandmothers and flirtatious couples.

Tati's defense of a humane society, eloquent and convincing, strikes the reflective viewer as rather futile. He is what Horace called a *laudator temporis acti,* one who sees the past through a rose-colored lens. It is no secret that he prefers the much plowed but fertile soil of older European traditions to the more synthetic, sleek Astroturf of secular technocracies. Who can forget the charming old lady at the end of *The Big Day* and her remark that "it is not the Americans who make the wheat grow." Nor, Tati seems to say throughout the canon of his works, is it the Americans who make personalities grow. In *Mr. Hulot's Holiday* and *My Uncle,* most of the adults who surround Tati are distinctly less human and warm than he. Despite his angular, sporadic gestures and giraffelike gait, his transcendence over the environment in terms of spontaneity, involvement, and colorfulness casts long shadows on those around him. Like the protagonist of *Il Sorpasso*, they are people leading Thoreau's "life of quiet desperation," but within the newer compulsive pressures of the industrial cycle of "work-consume-rest."

Tati's films offer cogent theological insights for those capable of deciphering them within the strange syntax of his mimetic, marionettelike performance. Upon penetrating the various strata of humor, social philosophy, and cultural prejudice (one detects in Tati a slight trace of "France über alles"), there appears a rich vein of theological ore. If I were to sum up the single most important cinematic religious insight in Tati's trilogy, it would be that the rate of spiritual growth can never fall much behind or advance much ahead of the social stream of expectations.

What happens when this social stream changes direction and with it the majority's set of expectations? We have had glimpses of this in *Potemkin*, *Hud*, *Il Sorpasso*, and *Charly*, as well as in Tati's films. Does one accommodate tactfully as in Luchino Visconti's *The Leopard* or does one wage war as the freedom-loving cowboy in David Miller's *Lonely Are the Brave?* Let us briefly compare these films, since they concentrate mainly on the psychological responses of determined, intelligent men faced with the collapse of structures that had earlier determined their personalities.

In *The Leopard*, Burt Lancaster plays the Count who must now adjust to the victorious entry of Garibaldi's "Red Shirts" into Sicily. The wave of liberal nationalist feeling in the *Risorgimento* movement will carry away with it the aristocratic, almost patriarchal, system of feudal landholdings, with its political control mechanisms and its support by the Church. But as history proves repeatedly, the disappearance of one form of social hierarchy only means its replacement by another. Whereas nobility and blood ties may count for less in the new order, wealth and marriage ties will serve to maintain in modified form the pyramidal nature of the old Sicilian society. The Count, forced to abandon his customary approach by authority, must now resort to diplomatic strategy. Only in this way will he be able to continue as an influential part of the unified, republican Italy. His success is guaranteed by his daughter's marriage to an *arriviste* of the pro-Garibaldi camp. The key note in Giuseppe di Lampedusa's novel is brought out patently by Visconti in his skillful direction of the film version: "The more things change, the more they stay the same."

As seen in *The Leopard*, a very effective social and psychological coping device is accomodation to change. However, it is not the only one; another is open resistance. In *Lonely Are the Brave*, Kirk Douglas masterfully portrays the cowboy who shears away barbed wire fences, assists "wetbacks" across the border, and escapes from prison in flight from a sheriff's posse and a military helicopter. He is one of the dispossessed of the earth, if not physically, then certainly psychologically. Burt Lancaster's Count can survive amid change without posing the kind of threat that causes persons like Anne Boleyn, Marie Antoinette, or Joan of Arc to be dispatched as dangerous. In so doing, he is not without influence, even in the new era of change. This is not the case with Kirk Douglas's cowboy, who has no way of being represented in the corporate, legislative, and other institutional decisions whose cumulative, unintended consequences deprive him and others of their spiritual birthright. In the face of inexorable social change, the options for remaining free narrow down to two for the great mass of humans: go down fighting or go down. Which is the better way—the way of the tragic cowboy hero in *Lonely Are the Brave*, hit while fleeing for liberty on his horse by a trailer truck delivering toilet fixtures, or the way of the alienated cowboy in *Hud*, dying by degrees amid lust, liquor, and cynical laughter while working for "The Far West Incorporated"? The choice, in either case, leads to harsh consequences.

An existential theology must address itself to this historical juncture with its vertiginous rate of social and technical change. If mankind wishes to find a guiding star by which to navigate its ship of destiny in the evening of the twentieth century, one way of setting its compass would be to learn from the abiding transcendental patterns of spiritual response as found in the plots of such films as *The Rules of the Game*, *Il Sorpasso*, *My Uncle*, *The Leopard*, *Lonely Are the Brave*, and *Hud*. These films on social change provide an invaluable service: they show the transient, precarious bases for human values and even for religious commitment. What Marx called "false consciousness," the logic people follow due to misunderstood premises of their peculiar societies, is true of religions in which the teachings of revelation or great spiritual masters are subtly transformed, often diluted, by culturally conditioned practices. Often religious bodies lose the "divine scent" of their primitive inspiration. Social change often acts to unmask the pretenses of "milieu religiosity," thus aiding man to find once again that lost scent of transcendence. A cinematic theology teaches us not only about the psychological consequences of social change in the lives of individuals but also about the spiritual alternatives of relief: convenience (e.g., the Count in *The Leopard*), capitulation (e.g., *Il Sorpasso*), courage (e.g., *Lonely Are the Brave*), caricature (e.g., *My Uncle*), corrosion (e.g., *Hud*), or the classical escape through philosophical detachment (e.g., Renoir's attitude in *The Rules of the Game*).

Finally, there is the problem of the psychodynamics of crowd behavior. What happens when suggestion-prone people assume an attitude and act upon it collectively in a time of crisis? Is man's transcendental reach operating in terms of rationality, altruism, and the search for truth? A cinematic theology presents a dark picture of this instance. Consider William Wellman's *The Ox-Bow Incident*, a film version of Walter Van Tilburg Clark's novel. Two cowboys suddenly find themselves in the throes of mob hysteria in a small frontier town in late-nineteenth-century Nevada. Word has just arrived of the murder of a rich cattleowner by three bandits. The embers of suspicion are fueled by boredom, ignorance, and xenophobia till a flaming hatred engulfs three strange men who are captured while sleeping not too far away from the scene of the reported crime. A kangaroo trial is quickly held and the men are sentenced to be lynched. After the lynching, it is discovered that there was no death and that the three dead men were not the bandits in question.

The lesson to be drawn seems to be that in moments of massive gatherings of people, the devil's hymns drown out the faint voices of the better angels of our nature. Stuart Rosenberg's *A Hall of Mirrors* is another warning against self-righteousness.

Paul Newman plays Rheinhardt, an ex-musician who becomes

involved with a right-wing radio station in present-day New Orleans. At a hate rally where Laurence Harvey, a fanatical religious minister, fans the embers of violence, Newman tries to intervene but too late. A riot breaks out and the mounted police arrive. The fury of unrestrained crowd passion is depicted in all its bitterness. The psychology of mob behavior is significant in this film for a cinematic theology since it shows how the subconscious workings of emotions, prejudice, and economic interests can disguise themselves behind the masks of democracy, prosperity, and religion. Extremist movements such as that in *A Hall of Mirrors* reveals the typical self-righteous assumptions of religious crusaders and political zealots. A similar treatment of ideological bias is found in Martin Ritt's *The Great White Hope*, a film about the racial prejudice faced by a Negro heavyweight champion in pre-World War I America.

In no way has Hollywood distingushed itself more than by drawing the public's attention to collective bigotry and crowd irrationality. One thinks of such films as *Fury, They Won't Forget, The Black Legion, Intruder in the Dust, To Kill a Mockingbird, The Cardinal, In the Heat of the Night*, and *Medium Cool*. The awareness of antitranscendental forces in crowd behavior is no mean achievement in a world in which more expressions of mob behavior will occur as population pressures increase and social tensions mount. Is it so unthinkable that conventional models of civic virtue—those noted for business integrity, industriousness, and church membership—could be overwhelmed by paranoiac fears and crusading zeal? And if such thunder on the political right is a threat, what of the millions upon millions of socially discontented persons who could be made to march lock step in a leftist revolt against the establishment? A relevant cinematic theology must acknowledge the domain of animal instincts and its role in impeding what Eastern Christian religions call the divinization of man through religion.

To synthesize these remarks in terms of a cinematic contribution to a behavioral theology, six basic propositions should be stressed. The first is the psychological release that imagination provides man in his attempts to transcend the constraints of environment. In *If . . .* we see three determined English schoolboys grow in their conviction that their military boarding school is irrelevant, an obstacle to progress, and damaging to the students, if not to the administration and faculty as well. The question of total institutionalization and its lateral consequences have rarely been as well considered, although there are other motion pictures that have succeeded in treating this theme: Jean Vigo's *Zero for Conduct*, Leontine Sagen's *Maedchen in Uniform*, Buzz Kulik's *Riot*, George Stevens' *The Diary of Anne Frank*, and Bryan Forbes' *King Rat*. If the demographic growth rate is projected onto a shrinking globe where time and distance barriers are being collapsed by technical advances, then such planetary pressures can simulate the conditions of total institutionalization. In this case there will be serious theological implications in massive flight through fantasy, imagination, and psychological escape values. We have already seen a preview of this (e.g., Otto Preminger's *Skidoo*, Dennis Hopper's *Easy Rider*, and Jean-Luc Godard's *Weekend*). To expect heroic responses from the plurality of people in situations demanding ever greater self-sacrifice is not a behavioral datum to be drawn from life as presented on the screen.

The second logical premise is that man's liberty can be completely short-circuited in certain extreme cases of hardship. Peter Lorre's role as the child rapist-murderer in *M* is a pathetic case study in psychic determinism. Of Lorre's heartrending apologia, "I can't help myself," Pauline Kael has said, ". . . it is one of the great, unforgettable cries of anguish."[2] Undoubtedly one of the most humanistic contributions of cinema has been its ability to awaken compassion for persons we are ordinarily prone to condemn without understanding their psychology as being a subjective form of logic, which rules all human behavior for better or for worse. This empathy, communicated impeccably in *M*, is found as well in John Ford's *The Informer*, Robert Bresson's *Pickpocket*, Pier Pasolini's *Accatone*, Federico Fellini's *The Swindler*, and in George Stevens' *A Place in the Sun*. The exercise of human transcendence is always a vector force of two component factors: man's interior disposition and his social history. The interiorization of *M*'s personal social history apparently extinguished all spark of psychic freedom: the instinctive grasp became the transcendental reach. This is conceivable in every human life ("There but for the grace of God go I").

The third principle is that a behavioral theology must sensitize human consciences to the unwitting but nevertheless real complicity in structures that limit the transcendental reach of those persons for whom social history is a crushing personal burden. Whenever man has the sensation of being "cabin'd cribb'd, confin'd," he will dream of escape, even if that means violently boring a hole into the protective walls society raises. In *High and Low*, the captured kidnaper confesses that he deliberately chose his victim because he lived ostentatiously in a big house on a hill. The psychology of the "have-not" is an idiosyncratic logic that society does not accept. The industrialist, however, wishes to understand more than society. Free of self-pity and detached from any vested interest, he pieces together the jigsaw puzzle in which his own figure emerges no less dark than that of the convict facing him. It then dawns on him and on the viewer that some rob by means of pistols, threats, and forced entry, while others rob by means of lobbies, bribes, legal loopholes, tax evasion, and astute meanderings through the maze of legal, fiscal, and administrative structures. *High and Low* is an unusual film, a type rarely seen in the West. It is one of the most muted, yet nonetheless devastating, critiques of modern industrial society, with its indifference to the larger web of social relationships and their incidence on personal lives. Kurosawa's film touches a cord deeper than mere social protest or psychological illumination; it replicates one of the oldest, most spiritual themes in literature, the ironic search of an Oedipus Rex who discovers he is the murderer of his own father. Such self-revelation is the indispensable first step toward religious insight. Small wonder that this shaft of wisdom comes from an Oriental bow, where self-knowledge is the basis for all spiritual progress!

Why is such self-knowledge so vital? Because without it, social expectations flounder at a low level and human potential remains aborted at many levels. When this is carried to an extreme, as in societies based on "rugged individualism," the saints, poets, scholars, and wise appear as deviants. Fred Zinneman's *A Man for All Seasons* is a superb example of how religious authenticity can be interpreted as treason. Equally illuminating for a redefinition of deviance according to a more spiritual frame of reference are Jacques Tati's films. We tend to relax our critical judgment in the case of Tati's role and see only a clumsy, clownlike figure. Perhaps it may really be that, putting aside his physical appearance and gestures, Tati is truly human, more human in fact, than the robotic types around him who pass for humans. It is really the others whose spiritual growth has been stunted, even though they respond as human beings in all the customary, superficial ways. Since there is only one Tati and many philistinelike folk, we may miss his orthodoxy because of the statistical weight of the conformists. Hulot, Tati's character, is exerting his transcendence continuously while the others pursue their assigned roles of routine service for social ends they never examine and so can never constructively criticize. In his three films—*The Big Day, Mr. Hulot's Holiday*, and *My Uncle*—Tati has waged a stirring crusade against the macro-determinism of those technological forces in blind search of a mission that no one as yet seems able to define clearly.

We have seen how spiritual development is somehow linked to the self-fulfilling prophecies that issue unconsciously from social structures to be inculcated in its members by the process called socialization. Thus the fifth principle becomes the impact on people of the new expectation patterns caused by swift social change. Insecurity is the first result for a person who, while remaining in identically the same place, becomes a "migrant in time." The cowboy in *Lonely Are the Brave*, the cowboy in *Hud*, the Count in *The Leopard*, and the car speedster in *Il Sorpasso* are insecure since their inner and outer worlds clash. While they cannot seriously go back, as Tati perhaps would wish, they are reluctant, like Chaplin in *Modern Times*, to go forward. What to do then—to change or not to change? By forcing options, social change reveals character, provoking counteraction (*Lonely Are the Brave*), compromise (*The Leopard*), confirmation (*Il Sorpasso*), or merely a curse (*Hud*). Cinematic theology reaches the peak of excitement at the point when it pursues the spiritual lifeline of a character over time, particularly during times of social quake.

The last principle concerns mass man in social crisis. Do crowds behave like persons with transcendental capabilities or like beasts who respond simply to pleasure-pain reflexes? The motion picture screen has presented scenes that are not easily forgotten: the Klan (*The Birth of a Nation*), the *Black Legion* (starring Humphrey Bogart), the irate lynch mob (*Fury, They Won't Forget, The Ox-Bow*

Incident, Intruder in the Dust, The Cardinal), ultra-conservative fanatics (*A Hall of Mirrors*), radical activists (*The Trial*), youthful protestors (*Wild in the Streets, Medium Cool,* and *Woodstock*), Nazi terrorists (*Frieda, Hangmen Also Die, The Diary of Anne Frank, The Pawnbroker, Judgment at Nuremberg,* and *Hitler's Last Ten Days*), and military brutality (*From Here to Eternity, Warhunt, The Thin Red Line, Home of the Brave, King and Country,* and *Paths of Glory*). These scenes are kaleidoscopic proof of the distrust man must cultivate regarding group action. While there is safety in numbers, dependency on crowd moods can be perilous. There is a sleeping tiger in each of us in terms of latent evil and lurking passion. Society can aggravate, frustrate, or tame these tendencies provided that society itself is being constantly reinforced by sources of transcendental energy and moral verve.

3

A Cinematic Theology of Freedom

JOHN FRANKENHEIMER'S *Bird Man of Alcatraz* depicts the true life story of Robert Stroud, condemned to life imprisonment in the renowned Federal penitentiary in San Francisco Bay. The protagonist, well enacted by Burt Lancaster, distracts himself from his confinement by a passionate interest in birds. This also allows him to curb a spirit of bitterness innate in his character. A very moving scene appears early in the movie when Lancaster's Stroud picks up a fallen bird on a rainy night in the prison courtyard. The presence of this living, warm creature in need touches a chord of compassion in the sentenced killer, thus beginning what is to evolve into an outstanding career as an inmate-ornithologist. Whereas his fellow prisoners allowed their lives, even their souls, to be directly shaped by the walls, bars, and prison guards, Stroud soared above them all—through his mind and imagination—as if he himself were a bird free to fly.

One of the consequences of this new-found "intellectual freedom" is the noticeable growth in Stroud. A revealing scene occurs, one whose full spiritual significance was missed by many viewers of the film. Busy with his research, Stroud is approached by a trustee prisoner, who, looking around to avoid notice, stealthily offers him a second helping of food. The steady glance that Stroud fixes on the prisoner is pregnant with meaning; it is a mingled look of compassion and scorn, for he sees the trustee as a double prisoner, spiritually as well as physically. Having accepted the "rules of the game," the trustee has lost human dignity, those transcendental powers of self-respect and honor which are the finest fruits of liberty. This scene is redolent of the couplet:

> Two men looked out of prison bars,
> One saw mud, the other saw stars.

We become what we behold, William Blake, has pointed out. The trustee has interests as base as mud, while Stroud, through his intellectual passion, sees stars.

One other powerful scene from *Bird Man of Alcatraz* deserves to be discussed: the confrontation between Stroud and the warden. The warden is a progressive man with a serious intent to rehabilitate. He is, nevertheless, committed to the paternalistic as-

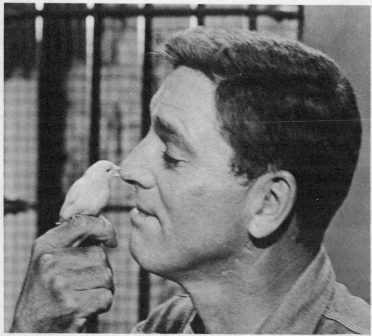

Courtesy: United Artists Corporation.

Burt Lancaster in *Birdman of Alcatraz*.

sumptions of the penal philosophy at work in virtually all state and Federal correctional institutions the world over. While paternalistic penology may be justified in the case of many prisoners, Stroud is certainly an exception. His self-confidence and dignity grow because he deals with life, the life of birds. Recalling incidents such as that of the trustee with the food, Stroud bluntly—for that is his manner—accuses the warden of being a failure, not so much as a warden but as an institutional symbol. Stroud's fearlessness in this scene exudes a spirit of freedom that elevates him in the viewer's esteem higher than in that of the warden himself, apparently a well-intentioned and basically a good man. Physically, the warden may be freer but there is little doubt that spiritually Stroud is by far the more free. The warden has freedom, but Stroud is free.

The most basic obstacle to freedom is the inability to move where one wishes, which is why the prison is the glaring symbol of human antipathy, a necessary evil that is progressively being mitigated in its harsher, more deterministic aspects. Freedom is a word that has gained great currency in this century. It is a chant that has been picked up by all minority groups of race, religion, and class, and more recently by workers, women, and even youth. Any discussion of transcendence must touch on the question of the conditions whereby man exercises his powers of autodetermination. Having examined some aspects of a behavioral theology through film documentation, we are now in a position to examine more closely why and how man is more than the sum total of influences that converge on him in time and space. Freedom, the condition *sine qua non* for history, politics, and art, is found at work in processes, not solely in acts. These processes are based on interpersonal and intergroup dynamics that are susceptible of influences from persons, particularly leader types. Once human beings choose to launch movements, to create institutions, to found governments, and to develop cultures, these in their turn shape man's future destiny. All exercises of freedom are basically choices among what determinisms man wishes to live under and struggle against.

Shackled human liberty is not restricted only to prison circumstances. It is likewise found in military dictatorships where national systems fall under the sway of some strong leader and begin to express designs of conquest on other nations, usually on small neighboring states. For instance, in *The Great Dictator*, Charlie Chaplin plays a Jewish barber who bears a remarkable likeness to Hitler. By force of circumstance he manages to substitute for the Nazi leader, providing humorous material for several scenes of mistaken identity. However, the comic strain is broken at the end of the film with an impassioned speech in defense of political liberty. Another example of the spiritual dimension of liberty in political repression systems is David Lean's film of Boris Pasternak's Nobel Prize-winning novel, *Doctor Zhivago*, based on Robert Bolt's screenplay. The Russian Revolution is the backdrop whereby Zhivago gains insight into himself as neither saint nor hero but as a weak man who must face the political cancer and meaninglessness of his society. This he manages, not by despair nor indifference, but by humility and love. Referring to Pasternak's masterpiece, Thomas Merton wrote:

Nowhere in Pasternak does one get the impression that his heroes are up a blind alley, beating their heads against a wall. . . . Pasternak sees the blind alley and sees the wall, but knows that the way out is not through the wall, and not back out by the way we came in. The exit is into an entirely new dimension—finding ourselves in others, discovering the inward sources of freedom and love. . . .[1]

In the film *Your Excellency*, the Mexican comedian Cantinflas plays a United Nations ambassador from a tiny republic in Latin America. Needing his crucial vote on a pending issue of vast international significance, two large powers, Dolaronia and Los Verdes, try to obtain his support. Obviously caricatures of the United States and Russia, the representatives of Dolaronia use economic incentives while those of Los Verdes try seduction and intrigue. The stirring scene comes at the end when Cantinflas tells the astounded members of the General Assembly that he has resigned as ambassador and so cannot vote. He then speaks of the counsel of Christ to "Love one another" and how in practice, nations interpret this as "Enslave one another." Pronouncing a curse on both great powers and admonishing all the countries present for escalating suspicion, distrust, and hate, Cantinflas leaves the podium. As at the ending of Chaplin's *Modern Times*, he walks down the path arm in arm with the girl he loves. Again a spark of transcendence has been struck from the surface friction of political groups.

It cannot be denied that there are unjust social, economic, and political conditions that tend to demoralize man and to shrink the horizon of his opportunities of realizing some transcendental meaning in life. While this never eliminates the possibility of a heroic response, perhaps martyrdom, there is another form of transcendence: protest. The revolt of the three English schoolboys in *If . . .* has already been discussed as the exercise of countervailing power against a fossilized educational structure whose harmful hidden effects overshadowed its expressed noble purpose. There is an evangelical basis to political activism, as Jean Paul Paupert has shown in his book, *The Politics of the Gospel.* [2] Movies such as *If . . .* can provide a concrete basis for theological speculation on the right of individuals and groups to defend their freedom.

No finer cinematic contribution to a political theology as it bears on the rights of human freedom exists than Sergei Eisenstein's *Potemkin.* Protesting over the decaying meat offered them at mess, the sailors on the battleship Potemkin mutiny. Through the poignant burial service of the rebel leader at Odessa, the city comes to the support of the sailors by sending them food. With the success of the mutiny, the czarist troops appear to subdue the sympathizing exhilarated townspeople who have gathered on Odessa's steps. The isolated battleship then prepares to do battle with the entire Russian fleet, which joins them amid a burst of cheers from the sailors. In classic form, Eisenstein portrays a decisive event of the 1905 revolution: the oppression of the Czar and the irrepressible spirit of ordinary people. [3] The fact that this film has been voted the finest film ever made by an international poll of critics indicates its universal appeal beyond the ideological motives that prompted its production. Like the great Russian works of Dostoevski, Tolstoi, Solovyev, Berdyaev, and Pasternak, *Potemkin* holds out hope to man that he can resist tyranny. The inspiration derived from *Potemkin* has deeper theological than political resonance. It is a metahistorical experience, the spirit of man as the judge of outworn, unjust social structures.

Haskell Wechsler's semidocumentary film *Medium Cool* is also a study of that negative exercise of freedom called protest. It treats the 1968 Democratic National Convention in Chicago and the protest tactics of the hippies and yippies in Grant Park. Whereas the cheering townspeople of Odessa had no television camera focused on the brutal treatment they received from the state, the youthful protesters in Chicago skillfully used the photographers and television cameramen as allies in unveiling what they considered the abusive measures of Mayor Richard J. Daley's police force. It has been said that the camera can betray inadequate, even dishonest, leadership. This seemed to be the strategic assumption around which the protest movement organized its tactical campaign. As the police arrests and clubbings were transmitted to over 50 million U.S. television viewers, the protesters are seen in *Medium Cool* chanting in unison: "The whole world is watching! The whole world is watching!" However one regards the merits of the protest, the Chicago riots as much as the Potemkin mutiny were witnesses to the transcendence of man in resisting alleged abuses of state authority.

In this context, *Rebel Without a Cause,* starring James Dean and directed by Nicholas Ray, should be cited. The film, a melange of actual adolescent case problems in psychoanalysis by Dr. Robert Lindner, considers the vulnerability, the incomprehension, and the fierce pride of a teenager. As played by James Dean, we come to believe in the efforts of this one person to cut through the hypocritical social structures that have no relevance to contemporary youth. Dean's youthful rebel is in the same revolutionary tradition as Eisenstein's mutineers of the Potemkin and the Chicago demonstrators, all ready to stake their lives in the cause of remaking the world into a freer and more kindly place to live. *Easy Rider* is yet another example of a form of the search for freedom.

Films dealing with the protests of youth illustrate another principle in cinematic theology: awareness of constraints on freedom have undeniable social origins and are seldom found in isolation. While this is particularly true of impressionable youth in an outer-directed world of taste-makers and opinion-holders, the greatest influence on youth is that which they exercise mutually upon one another. For example, in William Wyler's film *Dead End*, not only lowly environmental conditions but also peer-group influences are at work. The Dead End kids, as they were later called, represented the "gang age" syndrome where transcendental ideals, innate in youth, can easily be stunted in their realization. The code of the street is dramatized in one scene where one Dead End kid threatens to cut a scar across the cheek of an alleged informer as the "mark of the squealer." How impressionable unschooled youth can be is seen from the awe among these East Side delinquents toward Baby Face Martin, played by Humphrey Bogart. As they idolize him, one wonders whom he idolized at their age.

Earlier crowd psychology was treated as a chronic expression of man's "downward resourcelessness." In speaking of peer-group pressure we are between that massive annihilation of human liberty involved in all mob hysteria and the narcissistic "daydream" world of Peter Lorre's M. Youth, as it congregates to form social subsets, tends to act in a middle zone between crowd behavior and psychic infantilism. Some interesting case studies could be made of peer-group influences as seen in *Shoeshine, The 400 Blows, Expresso Bongo, The Explosive Generation, The Wild One*, and *The Leather Boys*.

In addition to outer social circumstance, there is also personal passion, not so much the criminal lust of a Peter Lorre in *M*, clearly psychically determined, but rather of Trina's hoarding tendencies in *Greed*, of Gypo Nolan's cupidity in *The Informer*, of the erotic weakness of the schoolmaster in Sternberg's *The Blue Angel*, of Eve's ambition to replace the aging star in *All About Eve*, of Fast Eddie's overconfidence in *The Hustler*, and of James Tyrone's stinginess in *Long Day's Journey into Night*. The motion pictures have illuminated the varieties of human flaws and moral fallibilities. This has been true even of nations such as was shown in Leni Riefenstrahl's documentary of Nazi pride during the 1934 Nuremberg Rally (*Triumph of the Will*). Later I shall discuss the more vicious and seemingly diabolical forms of corruption. Here I wish to treat the question of the crack in character that widens progressively till it engulfs the protagonist in a cataclysm.

Consider the film, *The Prime of Miss Jean Brodie*, directed by Ronald Neame. As played brilliantly by Maggie Smith, Miss Jean Brodie is a teacher in a Scottish private school. Conscious of her own pedagogic style, she stamps her pupils as distinctive Brodie "gir-r-r-ls." Her teaching is slanted toward fascism, utopianism, personalism, and dogmatism. Not only does she not examine her own assumptions, she arbitrarily teaches what she deems significant, thus exempting her personalized curriculum from any control by the school officials. She plays with the lives of her girls as with checker pieces, all the while seeing herself as liberal, openminded, and a willing candidate to become an educational martyr for her girls and the cause of progressive education.

The fatal flaw in Miss Brodie is that of the academician and the religious perfectionist, the belief that logic and idealism can change the world. Meanwhile, she herself is struggling to meet her own emotional needs, even to the point of having an affair with the music teacher whom she obviously does not love. The most tragic effect of her viewpoint is seen in the death of one of her pupils, who goes to Spain to fight in the Civil War. Miss Brodie's attitude is not changed; she merely holds up the misguided girl as an example to the others. Underneath the mannered behavior of this dynamic woman is a deep authoritarian streak, a reluctance to share other's views, a tendency to use people, a lack of scruples about leading a double life.

The question of when are we free is not one we ourselves can answer. Miss Brodie believed herself to be free of unconscious forces of determinism—emotional, psychic, and social. By contrast, Peter Lorre's murderer in *M* knew he was not free. The first step to preserve freedom or to regain it, if partially or wholly lost, is to know both the subliminal and surface pressures, that operate against the exercise of liberty. The problem of passion in human behavior is one that often is treated in cinema from a legal, medical, and psychoanalytic viewpoint in such films as Pierre Chenal's *Crime and Punishment*, Edward Dmytryk's *Crossfire*, Richard Thorpe's *Night Must Fall*, Richard Fleischer's *Compulsion*, Richard Brooks's *In Cold Blood*, Robert Siodmak's *The Devil Strikes at Night*, and George Stevens's *A Place in the Sun*.

Less frequently do directors explicitly seek to interpret a film in religious categories. While such an act would be to sell their artistic birthright for a "pot of message," the sheer visual presentation of human lives in depth organizes itself in the eyes of the theologically sensitive viewer as a comment on human transcendence or the failures thereof. A good example is Billy Wilder's *Sunset Boulevard*, a baroque tale of an aging screen star, her butler (once her husband

and director), and a handsome but broke scriptwriter for whom she becomes patron and paramour. How to explain the Svengali-like hold which former silent screen actress Norma Desmond, played by Gloria Swanson, has on a handsome young script writer? Pauline Kael, admittedly no theologian, gives a very perceptive moral diagnosis of the parasitical decline of the central character played by William Holden. She describes him as a decent, charming and casually cynical young man, adding that he is "trapped at first by curiosity and fascination, then by his weakness, and finally by his humanity (he tries to leave but Norma attempts suicide).⁴ A behavioral theology, as noted earlier, should concentrate on both motive and deed. What is interesting in Miss Kael's description is the way the "downward resourcelessness" of William Holden's writer takes place: at first an innocent acceptance to work on a script, then an emotional involvement (more of pity than of love), and finally a decision to sever the sickening relationship. It is this decision that causes his own murder. While at no step of the way is he bound by external bonds, the "forg'd manacles" are psychic. Thus we feel the tragedy of Holden's senseless death much more keenly than that of, say, Peter Lorre's *M*. We view the M's demise as a blessing, the death of a human turned animal, but we lament the death of William Holden's character as that of a man with untapped human potential.

If there are structured weaknesses within human beings that impede a true exercise of liberty, there are also institutional debilities that draw tight circles around the transcendental possibilities of the human situation. *The Sound of Trumpets* is a classic film study in how the toils of bureaucracy can reduce the aspirations of a young man. Directed by Ermanno Olmi, we see a lad, played by Sandro Panzeri, obtain a post in a large corporation in Italy's bustling and industrialized North. The film is not interested in social reform but is content to show the character of this youngster as an individual. He is seen with his family, with a girl he meets at a competitive examination, with fellow workers in the office. As the film ends with the boy seated at his desk, we realize that all the multiple latent identities in him will be suffocated by the clerical drudgery of years and years until he will accept the task at hand without considering the end it may serve. His destiny is mirrored in both the resigned faces and robotlike motions of the older office workers.

In a more comic vein, Charlie Chaplin tried to capture the tedium of work on the assembly line in *Modern Times*, which directly confronted the implications of quantifying the work process. René Clair's *À Nous la Liberté* and Jacques Tati's *My Uncle* were similar attempts to satirize one of the pivotal techniques in Western civilization. Often commercial films do not care to put the glare of the spotlight on the neuralgic points of an economy with which it enjoys solidarity. For that reason, the industrial-economic constraints on liberty are often treated obliquely or with tongue in cheek. The astute movieviewer would not find it hard to deduce the hidden personal costs of socioeconomic systems in such films as *Bachelor Party, Boys' Night Out, On the Waterfront, La Notte, The Apartment, Days of Wine and Roses, Patterns,* and *Death of a Salesman.* Freedom can never be an absolute term, only a function of outer and inner conditions that are not, at times, always present in the proportions desirable to insure spiritual growth.

Finally, there is the act of freedom itself, best illustrated by the giving away of one's freedom in a gesture of freedom. In John Ford's *The Prisoner of Shark Island*, Dr. Roger Mudd, played by Warner Baxter, is sentenced to prison for having tended to the broken leg of John Wilkes Booth, Lincoln's assassin. A true story, *The Prisoner of Shark Island* presents us with a man whose dedication to his profession extinguishes any trace of bitterness, self-pity, and vindictiveness. This film, together with *Bird Man of Alcatraz*, is a paean to freedom in the deepest sense of the word. It would be rewarding to contrast both films with *Angels with Dirty Faces*, in which James Cagney plays a killer who goes to the electric chair screaming from fear. This cowardly act is in deference to the request of his priest friend, Pat O'Brien, who wants to disillusion the younger gang members of the parish from modeling their lives on his. Freedom in these films goes much deeper than mere liberty of motion.

These are examples of consciously free people who live outside the zone of psychological twilight, where human actions are ethically ambiguous. The films of Akira Kurosawa are also invested with this moral lucidity. In *Sanshiro, Stray Dog, High and Low, The*

Seven Samurai, Yojimbo, and *Red Beard,* black and white are sharply delineated. The free man for Kurosawa is not necessarily he who acts virtuously but he who recognizes when he does not. Many Western films share this same quality of moral intuition and respect for those frontiers of freedom that protect other's rights: George Stevens's *Shane,* Fred Zinneman's *High Noon,* Howard Hawks's *Red River,* John Ford's *Stagecoach,* John Huston's *The Misfits,* Sam Peckinpah's *Ride the High Country,* and David Miller's *Lonely Are the Brave.*

The victory of freedom is in a self-chosen form of death that could be averted only through some personal compromise. The film par excellence to illustrate this is Carl Dreyer's *The Passion of Joan of Arc.* Played by Falconetti, Joan is cross-examined five times as we are given close-ups of her and her inquisitors. The camera angles

Copyright © 1966 Columbia Pictures Corporation.

Paul Scofield in a scene from the Columbia Picture *A Man for All Seasons.*

provide a startling new language of profiles, emotions, glances, and attitudes. In *Classics of the Foreign Film*, Parker Tyler describes the consequences of Joan's courageous decision to face death rather than to be disloyal to her voices: "The peasant spectators, who have reviled and cursed Joan, break down, weeping and rush from the scene as though whipped by the billowing smoke: the world's judgment has been brought to its knees because a human individual, in the greatest pain, has risked all she had to risk."[5]

Another film that treats a state execution as the moment of religious truth is *A Man for All Seasons*, based on Robert Bolt's successful play about St. Thomas More. Fred Zinneman, the director, has added another fine trophy to his treasury of films dealing with individual freedom and integrity (e.g., *From Here to Eternity*, *High Noon*, and *A Nun's Story*). More's character is portrayed early in the film when he unequivocally and with quiet assurance states his position: "It is not important what is believed, rather why one believes." Could this be the key premise of a transcredal religious ethos? Neither More's daughter, Meg, nor his wife, Lady Alice, can dissuade him from a stand that will lead to his destruction. So upright is More that Henry VIII wanted his reputation as an ally. More's objectivity of commitment in the "hell-broth" situation in which he found himself is admirably played by Paul Scofield.

In summarizing a cinematic theology of freedom, the following principles can be ascertained. The first is that "bars do not a prison make" but rather the interior disposition of the person involved. Related forms of coaction were seen to be only extrinsic impediments to human transcendence in *Bird Man of Alcatraz*, *The Great Dictator*, *Doctor Zhivago*, and *Your Excellency*. Man's response is what stamps his character and his milieu.

A second modality of freedom is that of protest under certain conditions of authoritarian oppression, as in *If . . .*, *Potemkin*, *Medium Cool*, and *Rebel Without a Cause*. In each of these films there was a grievance against legitimate authority. The implications of a political theology are interesting and worthy of further study, especially for those who believe that a nonviolent theology does not exhaust the meaning of the Gospel. As we know, the word "protest" forms part of one of two mainstream currents of Christianity.

Related to this is the influence exercised by members of a group upon one another, expecially in protest movements and most especially in the case of youth. Some fascinating case studies of peer-group psychodynamics and its moral implications are found in *Dead End*, *Shoeshine*, *The 400 Blows*, *The Wild One*, and *I Vitelloni*, to name a few of the more pertinent films. Basically, they show that youth tend to direct their vertical transcendent energies into horizontal channels of "in-group" goals and attitudes.

The fourth principle of a cinematic theology of liberty states that freedom is never stronger than the moral weaknesses of the person exercising it, especially as manifested in passion. The film industry has left us a veritable mine of examples to choose from in this area, among the more memorable instances being *Greed*, *The Blue Angel*, *All About Eve*, and *The Hustler*. The Greeks had a word for the unraveling of personal destiny due to a character flaw: *amartia*, a word whose usage has been consecrated by critics of tragedy ever since. The *amartia* is not only found in people but in groups as well (*The Triumph of the Will*). The most tragic consequence of blind passion is that which leads to the death of the innocent, as in *The Informer*, *The Prime of Miss Jean Brodie*, and *Sunset Boulevard*.

The fifth principle relates to the weight of institutional disabilities on individuals who work within them. Singled out for discussion were *The Sound of Trumpets*, *Modern Times*, *À Nous la Liberté* and *My Uncle*. Later, in a different theological context, other plots concerning bureaucratic obstacles to human transcendence will be discussed: Fred Zinneman's *A Nun's Story*, Alexander Mackendrick's *The Man in the White Suit*, Orson Welles's *The Trial*, and Gordon Douglas's *The Detective*. These films spell out the implications of the growth of rational organization in size and complexity as heralded by Max Weber, the German cultural historian. Weber foresaw how social options for exercising transcendence would be progressively narrowed down. Film has treated cases of extreme reaction to this process: the social pariah, as in *Easy Rider*, the martyr such as Anne Frank in *The Diary of Anne Frank*, or the misunderstood charismatic Pope in *The Shoes of the Fisherman*.

The ultimate in freedom is the freely chosen way of death for a conviction. The victory over death, always ambiguous in the life and death of the overwhelming number of persons, is beyond doubt in the case of religious martyrs such as a St. Joan of Arc or a St.

Thomas More. The transcendence referred to constantly in this book is incorporated into history through concrete people, places, and events, all bearing a name, a place, and a time. These are not legends, no matter how legendary their lives may seem to us. In the chapter on redemptive sacrifice I shall return to this question of freedom despite death.

4

Conscience, the Transcendental Referee

IN THE TRIAL proceedings of St. Joan of Arc, used by Carl Dreyer as the basis for his silent film masterpiece, *The Passion of Joan of Arc*, we read about those "voices" that sent the country maid first to visit the Dauphin, and then to lead the French army against the British. In a certain sense, these were voices of conscience revealing concrete imperatives. Similar voices were heard by St. Thomas More (*A Man for All Seasons*). He is reported to have once said to a person who urged him to submit to Henry VIII's will: "Your conscience will save you; my conscience will save me." What can cinema say about this strange force, conscience, which in a pluralistic world demands objective rules of tolerance for subjective norms of commitment? If the voices are varied, even contradictory, can they all equally lay claim to having issued from a single higher source of transcendental inspiration? This dilemma, a stumbling block for many, appears in film. Cinema furnishes some solid inferences for relating religious freedom with that form of transcendental determination (not determinism) called conscience.

The clearest presentation of the problem is seen in Robert Bresson's *Pickpocket*. Unfortunately, the films of Bresson are only known to a small coterie of art-film patrons in the United States. The plot of *Pickpocket* is simple: a young, modest man learns the art of wallet-lifting, a deft practice whose rewards are as risky as they are uncertain. His motive is to help first those of his immediate family, especially his mother, and secondly other needy people. This latter-day Robin Hood is suspected by a police official whose personal curiosity is piqued by the career of a person who obviously has chosen his métier with a purpose. A go-between arranges a meeting in a public bar and the conversation is directed discreetly to thievery as a vocation. The pickpocket's argument rests on the social utility of altruistic robbery on the grounds that maldistributed wealth could be better allocated. When the detective poses the logical question of what norms would influence these robbers in deciding whom to help, the pickpocket, with quiet assurance and conviction, replies: "Their conscience." The question of a larger immorality, condoned by society, is touched in this strange, subtly spiritual film, reminiscent of the end of Kurosawa's *High and Low* when the industrialist recognizes his own subliminal complicity with a harsh individualist ethic of acquisitive industrial societies.

Like *Pickpocket*, Fred Zinneman's *A Nun's Story* is a tale of a

Courtesy: New Yorker Films.

Robert Bresson's *Pickpocket*.

loner, a sister who no longer can accept the original raison d'être of her religious vocation. Hers is also a negative conviction that whatever else she may do in life one thing is clear: her inability to participate in her social institution as it is presently structured. Audrey Hepburn deftly plays the role of the sister whose missionary assignment in Africa becomes the occasion for a reassessment of her commitment. Zinneman's art comes to the fore in the final scene when the former sister receives civilian clothes and baggage in the convent and then leaves by the back door issuing out onto a forlorn alley. Here are the same mingled emotions of compassion and admiration felt in the key scenes of *Pickpocket* and *High and Low*. There are many who consider any impeachment of a social structure as a kind of flirting with anarchy and chaos. Many defenders of conscience stop short of questioning a social system's right to marshal the energies of its members for whatever cause it may deem right. Artists, often without intending it, shape conscience, thus serving as agents of moral suasion.

Motion pictures such as *A Nun's Story* often play this role of artistic and moral witness in the matter of conscience versus institutional arrangements. One may object that the voice of a Joan of Arc or of a Thomas More are of a different spiritual pedigree from that of the protagonists in *Pickpocket* and *A Nun's Story*. That is true. However, the more fundamental issue is not one of whether subjective conscience is right but rather whether objective intolerance is wrong. Man has only been given one normative aptitude—conscience. While each social system, culture, and subculture has ample means to defend itself against anarchy and other threats, the individual has only one sovereign defense—conscience. Many tragic conflicts arise from the collision course in which both society and conscience find themselves on specific issues. The presumption must always be that the abuse of a right of conscience open to social controls never nullifies the use of that right.

One case is that of *The Court Martial of Billy Mitchell*, which starred Gary Cooper as the ill-fated U.S. Army Colonel who foresaw the coming importance of air power. Today Billy Mitchell is considered a far-sighted pioneer and an American hero, but his actions were earlier deemed insubordination. It has been facetiously said of militaristic organizations that they do not bless the banners that go out to do battle but only those which come back victorious. The case of Billy Mitchell is akin to that of Joan of Arc, about whom Parker Tyler said: "Observe that the Church, after burning Joan at the stake, was moved to revive her as St. Joan."[1] Conscience, indeed, as Shakespeare noted in *Hamlet*, does make cowards of us all.

The issue of conscience becomes acute in films about persons within totally institutionalized situations such as the military. In Bernhard Wicki's *The Bridge*, we witness a brutal tale of callow German youths who, having been called up at the end of World War II, find themselves defending a bridge against an inexorable Allied advance. Just like the pupils in *The Prime of Miss Jean Brodie*, these lads have been encouraged with the inflated talk of idealism. They hold their ground through conscience, through the rigorous belief that this is what is required of them to serve "Das Volk, Das Vaterland und Der Fuehrer." The tragic loss of these young lives is due to an illusion of conscience, thus raising important doubts regarding blind, unquestioning obedience. For example, to what extent should youth accept society's norms? Director Nicholas Ray has handled the theme of youth's tortured conscience in its idealistic conflict with society in his films *They Live by Night*, *Rebel Without a Cause*, and *The True Story of Jesse James*.

The military conscience, internalized by years of careful conditioning, is a common theme of motion pictures. An example is the film of the Russian director, Grigori Chukhrai, *The Forty-First*, set against the background of the Caspian Sea in the civil war of 1920 between the Red Army and the White Army. Among the retreating twenty-three Red Army soldiers is a crack rifleman, Maria Bossova, who has shot forty of the enemy. When a White Army officer surrenders to her group, she is put in charge of him. As in *Heaven Knows, Mr. Allison* or *Two for the Seesaw*, the same plot elements exist: a couple, each with divergent commitments, who enrich one another through the mystery of mutual sexual attraction. She cares for him when he falls ill with fever; they make plans to live quietly in a Caucasian villa; they quarrel when she insists on being faithful to the Revolution. She grows melancholy. Finally they see a sailboat and jump for joy. It is a vessel with White Army soldiers. The prisoner runs to greet his comrades-in-arms while the female guerrilla shoulders her rifle in a blind reflex of obedience to the commissar's command to shoot any fleeing prisoners. After she fires, the prisoner falls into the water. Suddenly awakened to the full implication of what she has done, she runs toward him and cradles him in her arms, weeping over her dead lover.

This same Pavlovian type of military "conditioned reflex" is present in David Lean's *The Bridge on the River Kwai*. Alex Guinness plays the textbook officer who never doubts the code that formed him or the cause for which he is fighting. This lack of perspective has the characteristic of a Greek tragedy, for he loses the larger view of what he is actually doing. Having worn down the will of the Japanese commanding officer, played by the silent-screen star, Sessue Hayakawa, he has his men maintain their morale by building a bridge under his, not Japanese, direction. This micro-victory, undeniably gained by heroic courage, is canceled in the final scene when the British troops led by an escaped prisoner (William Holden) destroy the bridge. The irony is not lost on the astute viewer, who sees two allies fighting over their own precarious view of service to their country. The clash of consciences bent on attaining diverse patriotic goals is movingly presented. Does the end hallow the means? Who establishes policy regarding ends? When do subordinates fail in their acceptance of immoral commands? When should orders be questioned, if ever?

These questions, unanswered in *The Bridge On the River Kwai* (because never really raised explicitly), are the central theme of Stanley Kramer's *Judgment at Nuremberg*. The film used guest stars to present a panoramic view of the social consequences of Prussian-type military obedience. As we now know, Nazi generals under orders from Hitler passed commands to lower-ranking officers, who responded with all the unquestioning cooperation of men who, dedicatedly and unthinkingly, collaborated to form a bucket brigade in order to put out a sudden fire. Kramer's film is cleverly designed to spell out the full implications of what was praised as military virtue. The resulting horror at both the personal and family levels is set in even harsher relief by the presence of the patriarchal judge (Spencer Tracy). What is the theological justification of such a trial, if any? Is it, as some held, merely a legal form of vindictiveness imposed by the victor? Or is it something deeper, a primordial respect deep in man's being for life and its concomitant rights? This film was an appeal to conscience not by those abstract political collectivities called states, but by flesh-and-blood persons who constitute society in its practical "day-to-day" affairs.

The logical extreme of a "heel-clicking" brand of prompt execution of orders is seen in Stanley Kubrick's satire, *Dr. Strangelove, Or: How I Learned to Stop Worrying and Love the Bomb.* In the film, Air Force Commander Ripper (Sterling Haydn), for no good political reason, orders the B–52 nuclear bombers to attack Soviet Russia. Apparently insane, the Commander is met with no opposition. Nor does he know that the Russians have a Doomsday Machine capable of destroying the enemy in instantaneous reprisal. Another comic but disturbing role is that of General Turgidson (George C. Scott), who sees the situation of reciprocal destruction in a less dim light. He is almost optimistic in pointing out that the Reds will lose 150 million people to the 10 or 20 million American losses. The tragicomic elements of this rose-colored nightmare are brought to a finish with a symphony of nuclear bombs accompanied by a sentimental lyric: Here the Reality Principle is an insane one just as in Mike Nichols's *Catch 22*, but with more dire ramifications, given the advanced weaponry with which any World War III will be waged.

The "conditioned conscience" is also found in other areas of life such as religion (*Lilies of the Field*), labor and management (*The Man in the White Suit*), and academic life (*The Prime of Miss Jean Brodie*). This type of conscience, however, is different from the troubled conscience that resents the system within which it must work. Edward Dmytryk's film of Herman Wouk's best-seller, *The Caine Mutiny*, shows a case of military insubordination. In this film Humphrey Bogart earned his third Academy Award for the role of Captain Queeg, the psychopathic commander of the minesweeper, *Caine*. In contrast to Queeg, incompetent, a bully and a coward, is the executive officer, Lieutenant Maryk, reliable and hard-working. Influenced by Lieutenant Keefer, Maryk soon becomes convinced that Queeg is both neurotic and irresponsible. Before he can side-step the crucial issue of conscience versus the system by a transfer, the *Caine* is tossed by typhoon-agitated waves. Queeg gives the order to head the ship away from the wind and holds to his com-

Alec Guinness and Sessue Hayakawa in a scene from the Columbia Picture *Bridge on the River Kwai.*

Henry Fonda in *You Only Live Once.*

mand in the face of Maryk's pleas that they will founder.

Rather than permit collective suicide, Maryk invokes Article 184 of the U.S. Navy regulations and temporarily relieves Queeg of command for alleged medical reasons. The ship and crew survive, but this does not prevent a court-marital for Maryk and his fellow officers. The defense lawyer, Barney Greenwald, secures an acquittal, since Queeg's condition as a psychically disturbed person is manifest to all.

The strange ending, however, has Greenwald accusing Maryk and the junior officers of disloyalty. The argument given is a non sequitur of the first order. Greenwald vigorously defends regular officers such as Queeg who, by maintaining American ships afloat in World War II, kept people like the Jews from being boiled down for soap as was his grandmother in Nazi Germany. In his novel Wouk is saying that it is not for the individual to question the system. Most Americans, as William H. Whyte, Jr., pointed out in *The Organization Man*, agree with this viewpoint.[2] Whyte's own creed is summed up as follows: "The central idea—that the individual rather than society, must be the paramount end—animated Western thought long before the Industrial Revolution or Calvinism, or Puritanism, and it is as vital and as applicable today as ever."[3]

A defense of this basic American proposition is given in one of the most audacious films Hollywood has ever produced—Robert Aldrich's *The Big Knife*. The scenario treats a hyper-sensitive, decent, but weak movie actor, Charlie Castle (Jack Palance), who is frustrated by the production system headed by Stanley Hoff (Rod Steiger). His wife, Marion (Ida Lupino), from whom he is separated, reproaches him for being a cog in the machinery of the Hollywood assembly line system and for having betrayed his earlier ideals. Despite his refusal to sign a seven-year contract, he succumbs to the authoritarian persuasion of the producer, leading to his wife's decision to begin divorce proceedings. She hesitates when Charlie pleads with her.

The conflict of conscience becomes progressively more acute as it becomes clear that producer Hoff is unscrupulous and will eliminate even by murder anyone who interferes with his plans. In this case, he has incriminating evidence concerning a car accident in which Charlie was driving while intoxicated. The weak Charlie, feeling trapped, kills himself—a victim of conscience, of personal weakness, and of a powerful economic system of control. Could all these three be the "big knife" that cuts down the Charlie Castles of this world? In effect, the knife that cuts Charlie's veins is only a physical extension of the inward moral hemorrhaging of his own cowardice and the ruthless butcher-shop tactics of a system dedicated to the mass production and distribution of fantasies. This film, severely criticized in the United States, was more positively received as a courageous—one might say "conscience-impelled—work in countries such as France.[4]

Another study of the corroding of conscience and therefore human personality is Richard Burton's "burnt-out" performance as Leamas, the espionage agent in Martin Ritt's version of John Le Carré's *The Spy Who Came In From the Cold. Time* said of this film: "While the gears of intrigue mesh, Burton's face projects more nakedly than the novel did that Leamas, believing in nothing, half believes in his own worthlessness.[5] The corruption of others already presupposes the corruption of oneself. Again, Henri Jacques Clouzot's *Wages of Fear* presents another cynical view of the impact of power on human conscience, namely, the power of U.S. oil interests in Latin America. This moral decay is subliminal insofar as the film's theological meaning rests on the money that four men can earn by driving trucks with high explosives. Either they rot in a torrid climate or risk their lives to earn their escape. Clouzot is insinuating that not only can desperate men be bought, but also that only unscrupulous men will dare buy them. Once again the "big knife" is confronted in all its levels of meaning.

What happens when conscience is blunted? In Jean-Luc Godard's *Breathless*, Jean-Paul Belmondo plays an imitation Humphrey Bogart—a car thief, Michel—who rushes impetuously from one activity to another. He is charming in his nonchalance: rubbing his lips, lifting women's skirts on the street, deflating truck tires, and robbing parking meters. Basically, he seems to have no quarrel with anyone—neither the police, nor society, nor anyone. He is a type of parachutist who welcomes any terrain that welcomes him, provided he does not have to stay. This is what worries his American girl friend Patricia (Jean Seberg), who gives him away to the police in the hope that he will flee and she will be rid of him. However, true to the Bogart persona he has adopted he refuses to go, and is shot down in the street by the police while Patricia watches. While he lies dying, Patricia rushes up to him; his last words to her, vulgar but in tune with his sentiments and her betrayal, are: "Tu es dégueulasse." The film ends with a close-up of Patricia asking the policeman: "Qu'est-ce que c'est que dégueulasse?"

Breathless is a world of anarchistic values, the same world Kubrick depicts in *Dr. Strangelove.* There as well the social order is repudiated, sex but not love is possible, and death lurks not far away. It seems that conscience is nothing more than a tone-feeling of body or emotional moods. This message, spelt out in *Breathless,* is derived from the Paul Muni, James Cagney, and Edward G. Robinson gangster films of the 1930s. *Breathless,* however, presents a studied case of mannered immorality absent in films such as *Scarface, Public Enemy Number One,* and *Little Caesar.* Strangely enough, the phenomenon of the calloused conscience has been recently portrayed in the case of representatives of the law. There is case of Jack Smight's *Harper,* in which Paul Newman plays the private detective whose personal advantages clash with public duty. He is contemptuous of all others, even himself: he inebriates a woman to obtain information; he returns to his estranged wife for a night's comfort and discards her the next day; he borrows a clean shirt from a suspect and while changing into it goads the person to tears and confession.

This same cruel stance is embodied in other law-enforcement roles, such as Kirk Douglas in *The Detective Story,* Frank Sinatra in *The Detective,* and Steve McQueen in *Bullitt.* That the movies of this decade have featured ambiguity of role seems evident when one recalls how audiences have tended to identify with the "antisociety types" in *Bonnie and Clyde, Midnight Cowboy, If . . . , La Chinoise, Easy Rider,* and *Catch 22.* It should be noted that this kind of psychological ambiguity, with no boundaries for good and bad, often leads to theological ambiguity, that is, a lack of any decisive point of view, a mere desire to see through situations without seeing anything postive. Many of these films have a subtle Manichaean taint to them; they do not take seriously a world that is imperfect and unfinished, satisfying themselves that the mere opposition to this world is equivalent to achieving the perfection and harmony it lacks.

This subtle position of neutrality as being a kind of innocence runs throughout three of the finest films to come out of the sixties: Tony Richardson's *The Loneliness of the Long Distance Runner*, Akira Kurosawa's *Yojimbo*, and Martin Ritt's *Hombre*.

In these films conscience serves the same function as that of a delicate balance wheel in a fine Swiss watch. With great precision, the hero makes sure he keeps his loyalties divided and his integrity pure. It is easy to belittle this type of alienation. Pauline Kael, for instance, refers to Paul Newman's role of a white man raised by the Apaches in *Hombre* as a "masochistic modern hero."[6] Why, one is tempted to ask? Can societies, growing more complex all the time, really permit clear loyalties, at least for those who reflect on their commitments? If one accepts with Herbert Marcuse the steady extension of the Reality Principle, with its stress on self-interest and an individualistic ethos, one may ask: How does human conscience reach for transcendence if all it can do is to identify with one of a welter of rival, often petty in-groups? Liberty of choice within nonfree systems is a specious form of liberty. Does not transcendence as expressed in conscience become thwarted when the choices are among different paths of inauthentic commitment? If so, then the temptation to be an outsider becomes great, as in the case of Hombre. Richardson's Colin Smith and Kurosawa's Sanjuro are, existentially speaking, cut from the same cloth as Martin Ritt's Hombre. Sanjuro has no use either for the sake or the tea merchants since both are petty and mercenary, while Colin Smith is equally unimpressed by the public school competitors in the race and the headmaster of the Bristol correctional institute for whom he is running. Basically, Colin Smith, Sanjuro, and Hombre are all outsiders whose consciences prevent them from ever becoming insiders. Here Pauline Kael's habitual powers of insight are especially illuminating when she says of *Hombre:* "Split in his loyalties, the half-and-half hero can observe the cruelties and misunderstandings of both sides, he's a double loner. . . ."[7]

Let us take a closer look at the "double loner" role. Hombre sides with the Indians but also speaks with and acts for the white man as well. Colin Smith, convincingly enacted by Tom Courtenay with a pocked, proletarian face, sees through the tweedy headmaster of the Borstal reformatory who is anxious that he beat a public school in an upcoming track meet. He halts before the finish line to allow himself a double luxury, that of giving the victory to a rich boy who really needs nothing and that of denying the paternalistic headmaster his sought-after trophy. In *Yojimbo,* an expert samurai, wandering about in the feudal break-up of nineteenth-century Japan, comes into a town where one faction is at odds with another concerning the control of the gambling concession at the local silk fair. One display of Sanjuro's swordsmanship convinces each side that his services are indispensable. He systematically proceeds to rid the place of everyone except a friendly townsman whom he cuts down from his suspended position and then leaves, saying, "Now there will be peace." For some peculiar, unexplained reason, youthful audiences identify with these "half-and-half" heroes, impaled on their consciences in a society where the choices are unappetizing, even when not narrow. This is not necessarily Manichaeism, with its polarization of the universe into good and evil; it seems rather an awareness that in life the options lie between two species of death: one through loneliness or one through spiritual asphyxiation.

The question of conversion due to conscience now arises, a theme superbly handled in John Ford's *The Informer.* Victor McLaglen portrays the powerful, slow-thinking Gypo Nolan in the time of the Irish "troubles." He betrays his best friend, Frankie McPhillips, for twenty pounds, the price of a boat passage to America. The revolutionary organization of which they were both members becomes suspicious and tracks him down. He escapes by brute force and is shot in pursuit. Crawling into a nearby church, he sees Mrs. McPhillips in a pew and, having obtained her forgiveness, dies in her arms.

What is theologically noteworthy is that repentance lies outside of society's competence to assess or accept. This is clear in *The Informer.* It also comes to light, if in a less moving way, in a contemporary remake by Jules Dassin. *Uptight* treats a Black Power group in Cleveland, Ohio, after the assassination of Martin Luther King, Jr. In both films, there is evidence of the Old Testament "lex talionis"—an eye for an eye, a tooth for a tooth. The religious sanctuary of inner purpose and heartfelt contrition is one not accessible to guardians of the public order, who only recognize the efficacy of punitive and deterrent measures. In Fritz Lang's film *You Only Live Once*, Eddie Wilson (Henry Fonda) plays an ex-convict who, while trying to go straight, is falsely accused of a bank robbery. He gives himself up at the insistence of his wife (Sylvia Sidney) but is sentenced to death due to incriminating circumstantial evidence. He breaks out of prison before the news of his pardon arrives from the governor. He is eventually killed, a man who, upon his release from prison, when asked if he would "go straight," replied: "I will, if they'll let me." Society preaches reform but one wonders how realistic are the opportunities that it affords the contrite ex-convict. Conversion of the human heart is a response to those voices mentioned earlier. It is a spiritual encounter with no other witnesses but God. The cinema has often stressed the power of personal commitment not only to what is socially unforceable, but also in the face of what is socially punishable.

A word about conscientious objectors is in order before closing. The Quaker religion is especially noted for its nonviolent tendencies. In William Wyler's *Friendly Persuasion* a Quaker family in Civil War southern Indiana faces the question of whether the Friends can fight the Rebels who come to raid. The mother (Dorothy McGuire) is determinedly against it; the older son (Anthony Perkins) is inclined to self-defense; the father (Gary Cooper) states his philosophy somewhere between the two positions: "Man's life ain't wuth a hill uh beans, less'n he lives up ta his own conshunce." The boy is eventually allowed to go and fight for his country and for his manhood according to his own lights.

Hollywood seems to enjoy putting the quaker nonviolence philosophy to the extreme test. In *High Noon*, the lone sheriff, (Gary Cooper) is protected from being ambushed when his wife (Grace Kelly), contrary to her Quaker scruples, puts a rifle to her shoulder and kills her husband's would-be assassin. Again, in Howard Hawks's 1943 film, *Sergeant York*, Gary Cooper plays the real-life Tennessee farmer who, when in uniform in the France of World War I, lost his nonviolent inhibitions and was decorated for killing some forty Germans. Granted the rigor of Quaker teaching, these films on Quaker people under stress indicate that conscience is capable of accommodating to environmental circumstances. This recalls the raging theological debate of the past decade in "situation ethics," or what is more popularly known as "the new morality."

What does a cinematic theology tell us about man's conscience as the transcendental arbiter of his exercise of liberty?

1. The plural, often contrary voices of conscience are man's only reference point for responding to life situations in a transcendental way, even though a given society or subculture may not concur. This is well brought out in *The Passion of Joan of Arc*, *A Man for All Seasons*, and *Pickpocket*.

2. Tolerance in matters of conscience is less encouraged and more apt to be denied in situations of total institutionalization such as convents (*A Nun's Story*), the army (*The Court Martial of Billy Mitchell*), and schools (*The Prime of Miss Jean Brodie*, and *If . . .*).

3. The Pavlovian type of "conditioned reflex" is a barrier to a genuine exercise of the transcendental conscience as much as the "subliminally managed conscience" discussed in *The Forty-First*, *The Bridge on the River Kwai*, *Dr. Strangelove*, *Catch 22*, *Judgment at Nuremberg*, *If . . .* , *The Prime of Miss Jean Brodie*, and *Lilies of the Field*.

4. Conscience cannot be compromised, either legally or psychologically, without loss of interior peace and self-esteem. We saw that Maryk, in taking the command away from Captain Queeg in *The Caine Munity*, not only performed a service to the crew and to the Navy in averting disaster but complied with his own sense of higher duty. On the other hand, Jack Palance's performance in *The Big Knife* feelingly records the tortured soul and eventual suicide of an actor who could not resist the personal and systematic pressures that his movie career exerted on conscience. Moreover, we saw how the calloused conscience, a degenerate product of an earlier tradition of rebel gangsters, has now invaded both sides of the law. Not only do we have the new amoral criminal (*Breathless*) but, judging from cinematic evidence, he is finding competition in the brutalized law agent (*Detective Story*, *The Detective*, *Harper*, and *Bullitt*).

5. In complex societies with a highly individualistic ethos and socially sanctioned acquisitive urges, conscience often produces

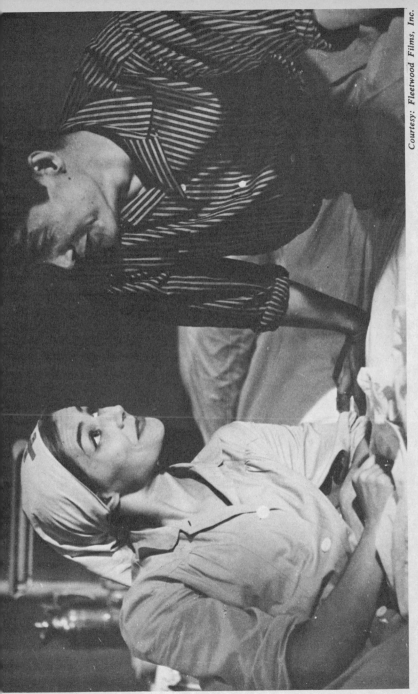

Alain Resnais' *Hiroshima Mon Amour.*

"half-and-half" heroes who feel compromised if they take sides definitely (*Hombre, The Loneliness of the Long Distance Runner,* and *Yojimbo*).

6. Conscience is a function of social circumstance leading to conversion. This can take many forms: either a death-bed repentance, or a movement away from lax conduct to a more transcendentally rigorous set of principles, or from a stringent code to an accommodated form of morality. The death-bed "turn" is shown in the moving film, *The Informer.* The conversion to a stricter way of life appears in films such as *You Only Live Once,* where social forces aborted the good intentions of the ex-convict. An accommodation of conscience to new, often extenuating, events can be seen in three revealing Gary Cooper films on Quaker morality: *Sergeant York, High Noon,* and *Friendly Persuasion.*

5

Toward a Cinematic Theology of Sex

As RELIGION is the point of convergence between human transcendence and divine reality, so human love is the horizon
where the transcendental reach of two persons intersect. Written
by a woman, Marguerite Duros, the script of *Hiroshima, Mon
Amour* bears a subconscious feminine viewpoint that may serve to
correct the undeniable subconscious masculine bias in theological
writings, even in the field of love and sex. Alain Resnais' film, a
pathbreaking effort in its treatment of interracial sex, merits the
serious consideration of theologians.

The film opens with one of motion picture history's stunning
scenes: the naked bodies of two lovers tightly intertwined with their
bodies glistening as if covered with phosphorescent sprinklings.
This is supposedly an after-image that symbolizes the radioactive
dust of Hiroshima. We discover that the woman is a French actress,
the man a Japanese architect. Later she tells him of her love affair
in 1944 with a German soldier who subsequently died on the day
of liberation. She had her head shaved and was locked up in a cellar
by her disapproving parents. Later she went to Paris on the day
Hiroshima was bombed. Although definitely in love with the Japanese, she is reluctant to yield to another experience that time is
certain to efface. For her, forgetfulness is man's lot. Just as she
outgrew the love affair with the dead German, so, too, the atomic
bombing of Hiroshima, she finds, has passed into oblivion for the
Japanese. The man admits finally that he too is beginning to forget.

The bittersweet quality of love in the post–World War II era has never been captured more tenderly. The crisis of human love depicted here is not one of inhibitions or psychological barriers; it is not one of moral censure or adverse public opinion; it is not one of absence of sincerity, nobility, or genuine love. What, then, is the theological valence of such a cinematic masterpiece? It lies mainly in the precarious nature of love as demanding a transcendental sign with personal, social, and divine references. Why does the architect admit his own transient emotional state? Why does the actress resist permanent surrender in the affair? Why has Resnais himself admitted that he had no particular liking for the heroine? Are there not deep psycho-theological reasons that the public, critics, director, and those within the industry have not yet plumbed as fully as they could or should?

Hiroshima, Mon Amour epitomizes the ambivalence of sex as do the films of Bergman, Buñuel, Fellini, Losey, Renoir, and Truffaut. In the past quarter-century movies have portrayed secularized forms so that the vertical upward pull of transcendence has been progressively translated into the horizontal attraction of lovers. Earlier this same leveling of transcendence was noted among the youthful peer-groups. This secularization process has performed one valuable function: it has made the love relationship autonomous in the strict psychological sense, thus counterbalancing such extrinsic considerations as puritanism in religion, parental conditioning based on false assumptions, and official school policies of sexual ignorance, all resulting in a puerile, often morbid curiosity among adolescents and emotionally immature adults. In this sense, secularization is all to the good. Indeed, it is a rare film that has appeared in the 1960s that has not dramatically advertised the emancipation of sex from ideological shackles. Even granting the abuses of this recent freedom against the discreet forms regarding intimacy, nevertheless, the screen, in general, has helped restore the imbalance that characteristically has been identified with the Victorian age of "prudishness and properness." The danger facing cinema is that it may easily go to another extreme and absolutize in its turn the newly won autonomy of sex. However, abuse does not argue against use. Film has helped toward a dynamic theology of sex.

A good example would be the film, *This Sporting Life*, directed by Lindsay Anderson. Frank Machin (Richard Harris) is a professional rugby player, very much a sensitive, confused, but strong type along the lines of Marlon Brando. The title is ironical since both rugby and sex are presented as pure antagonism. The love story unfolds between Machin and his puritanical landlady (Rachel Roberts). She rejects his insistent demands for a love she unquestionably feels but cannot give. His love needs a physical point of sexual encounter; her love must thrive on a platonic, nonmaterial plane. Writing in *Show* of Rachel Roberts as the frigid landlady, one writer has said, "She has created the definitive screen portrait of the Anglo-Saxon woman who has been taught that sexual happiness is wrong, who somewhere in her soul resents not the joy of others, but her own."[1] The allusion here is to sexual happiness, not to sexual libertinage. If the heroine had lived and had not been inadvertently killed by her lover, she doubtless, even in marriage, would have not found any peace in the matrimonial act. Anderson's film strongly suggests that sex as a valid human experience was not possible for her due to her past conditioning.

Cinema has also aided the public to appreciate virginity. Until quite recently, it has not treated with prurience the abuses of the vows of religious sisters, brothers, and priests. This promises to change with the appearance of a film such as *The Priest's Wife* in which Sophia Loren falls in love with a handsome clergyman (Marcello Mastroianni). There has been a policy of respect among moviemakers to portray clergy and religious as faithful to their state of celibacy. One thinks of John Huston's film, *Heaven Knows, Mr. Allison*, starring Robert Mitchum as a marine and Deborah Kerr as a nun. Stranded on a South Pacific island during World War II, both recognize the peculiarity of their situation. The marine is typical—alert, practical, resourceful, and not averse to pin-up girls, binges, and swearing. The nun is typical of a pre–Vatican Council Catholic religious sister—demure, intuitive, and cautious. The relationship between the two escalates naturally in the following psychological way: he refuses to let her surrender for his sake; he tries to obtain food from a Japanese commissary when he sees she cannot muster up courage to eat raw fish; she is concerned about his long absence and leaves the refuge of the cave; he makes a comb as a gift for her; she assures him that her vows are irrevocable; the next evening he proposes to her only to apologize the following day; he gets intoxicated the night she flees into the rain; he brings her back delirious; he obtains blankets but must kill the enemy to do so; three days later she is grateful, telling him that her flight was not from him but from the truth contained in his marriage proposal. The film ends with a landing of the American troops and Sister Angela promising the wounded Mr. Allison that he will always be her dear friend.

The significance of the film for a sexual theology is the maturing process each underwent in an improbable situation, fraught with tension and risk. Two sets of transcendental impulses resonate throughout the film: the desire for marriage and the commitment to total religious consecration. Since many people recognize from an early age which of the two vocations clearly attract them, it is not unusual for misunderstandings based on ignorance to arise with regard to the state that one did not choose. The truth of married love—the truth that Sister Angela never comprehended before—is not an absolute value, however autonomous its sexual basis. It seeks complementing in another form of equally true human commitment, namely, that of religious celibacy with its own independent basis in spiritual communion. That both Mr. Allison and Sister Angela part with closer ties of affection between them eloquently argues the theological premise that both sex and virginity, each in its turn, are positive movements within the same transcendental reach toward that which is greater than the human heart itself. This same truth is brought home in Fellini's *La Strada*, in the scene where Gelsomina and the nun share their common understanding of the two distinct modes each must adopt for serving and loving God, the latter as a virgin, the former by the side of Zampano. This divinization of love by celibacy and its meaning for humanity was also highlighted by Maurice Cloche's *Monsieur Vincent*, in which St. Vincent de Paul's chastity no less than his charity never appears as self-conscious superiority.

Let us explore the fuller spiritual implications of sexual love. In *Hiroshima, Mon Amour* there was a genuine bond of love, vibrant and thus ripe for consummation. Theologians in the past have not always treated the transcendental dynamic of a love affair apart from its moral attributes. The tendency in the past to categorize as

sinful led at times to a disregard of pastoral considerations in helping couples to sanctify—personally, socially, and religiously—their
union. What film has helped to do, especially since World War II,
is to bring to popular consciousness the irrevocable nature of
love experiences (recall the memory scene in *Hiroshima, Mon
Amour*) and their bitter aftermath when based solely on physical
attraction and passions (*This Sporting Life*).

The master taxonomist of sexual mores in filmdom is unquestionably Ingmar Bergman. His early films are not only psychologically
sound but sow many seeds of theological inference for the belief
that man and woman seek a continuing transcendental relation
beyond that assured by their own mutually rewarding union. In
Prison, Thirst, Summer with Monika, and *Summer Games*, Bergman explores the recovery process of couples who, after having
been drawn to each other by passion go through a psychic hell of
disillusionment and satiety.[2] In *Summer Games*, Marie, played
superbly by Maj Britt Nilsson, experiences the full gamut of sexual
love: that of first love as an adolescent, that of lovers seeking
novelty in neverending erotic games, and finally the mature expression of love by couples wiser through sorrow and experience. Bergman's insight is cogent for a theology of sexuality. For example, in
Hiroshima, Mon Amour, the man and woman are seen in transition
from stage two to stage three. When the film ends, their love,
physically consummated and as deep as ever, has still to ripen. This
is what gives the film its bittersweet quality.

Bergman has another contribution to make to a sexual theology,
namely, his remarkable ability to represent the female viewpoint in
love affairs. This is obvious in such films as *Women in Waiting*,
Summer with Monika, A Lesson of Love, The Dreams of Women,
and *Smiles of a Summer Night*. The last one is a classic film of upper
class manners, redolent of Renoir's masterly *Rules of the Game*. It
is worthwhile to consider this film not only because it is the best
compendium of Bergman's "rose period" philosophy of love, but
also because underneath the apparent gaiety is the theme of death,
a preferred Bergman theme to be discussed more fully later.

On the estate of the elderly Mrs. Armfeld, we meet an array of
people who are all psychologically disjointed in terms of their affections and social ties: Fredrick, the lawyer, is more compatible with

the actress Désirée Armfeld than with his child bride, Anne; while Désirée pleases the married Count, Anne by nature feels more at ease with Fredrick's son, the seminarian Henrik. Henrik, however, feels attracted to the flirtatious servant Petra, who sleeps with Frid the coachman. All in all, a series of overlapping liaisons occur in which duplicity, pleasure, and social posturing comport neatly with one another.

What are the "smiles of a summer night"? There are three that we know from our discussion of *Summer Games:* the first is for young lovers such as Anne and Henrik; the second smile is for the lighthearted, the frivolous, and the resigned such as Petra and Frid or the Count and Countess; the third smile is for the sad, the fearful, the confused, and the lonely such as Fredrick and Désirée.

As in Shakespeare's *A Midsummer Night's Dream* (William Dieterle directed this famous Hollywood movie), the players search for one another and their own identity. What stands out in Bergman's work is the immaturity and instability of the men. The women come off decidedly better in every respect, especially Désirée (Eva Dahlbeck). Is this a symptom of our atomic age civilization—the upsetting of the balance wheel that has traditionally ruled the sexes? Let us dwell a moment on this Bergmanian point, for it is a revealing one that reappears in David Lean's rendition of Boris Pasternak's *Dr. Zhivago.* There we see how much stronger Zhivago's mistress, Lara, is than Zhivago himself. Is woman, then, the womb to which man compulsively returns in a world where events seem too complex and baffling for him? The problem is a real one because it may be a tell-tale clue in favor of Marcuse's thesis that social psychology is displacing individual psychology. Certainly in the case of Zhivago, Lara represented at that crucial moment of meaninglessness in his life "the rain on the spotted window pane."

Lara helps Yuri Zhivago discover a fundamental metaphysical freedom which once regained leads him and her to put straight the psychological, social, and religious aspects of their relationship.

Just as in the case of freedom, love must also face boldly the question of both psychic and environmental impediments to the transcendental impulses of sexual communion. Martin Buber has given us fertile insights into the "I–Thou" relationship of love in general.[3] While his writings are easily applicable to sexual love, the historical development of the concrete psyche of an "I" or a "Thou" must also be considered. A complementary study of Buber's "I–Thou" should include such existential factors as culture, politics, and religion.

In the case of *Dr. Zhivago* we have such a complementary study. Against the broad and towering backdrop of the Russian Revolution is set a moving and highly intimate tale of "I–Thou." No one has dared to moralize about the fact that Yuri Zhivago is married and still in love with his wife. Lara, the "Thou" in the film, though seduced by Komarovsky in her girlhood, never ceases to symbolize for Zhivago or for the reader that spiritualization of love celebrated by Solovyev in *The Meaning of Love.*[4] This idealization of love is present in Pasternak's work. Robert Bolt, who wrote the script for Lean's film, observed that Pasternak "jumps absolutely obligatory material."[5] In the film we see the love scenes between Yuri and Lara. In the novel there is no reference to kissing or sexual relationships. We just discover in the course of reading that Lara gives birth to a love child, Tania, conceived in "the terrible years." Lara vanishes without a trace; Tania lives on, as Thomas Merton believes, "the Russia of the future."[6] Important is the chaste, undeniably mystical, lyricism of Pasternak's chronicles, reminding us of Solovyev's words that the mere primordial passion, if considered the primary condition of love, "makes love not only powerless against death, but itself inevitably becomes the moral grave of love long before the physical grave receives the lovers.[7]

This freedom, this transcendental fidelity, this divinization of a morally deviant relationship gives us a theological standard for appraising the quality of sexual love situations in the films. While keeping in mind the extramarital, but undeniably spiritualized, nature of the love union between Zhivago and Lara, a contrasting case should be studied, Michelangelo Antonioni's *La Notte*. His previous film, *L'Avventura*, presented the moral and cultural void of upper class Italians on a yacht cruise, for whom open sex like open air "serve as a shameless, bracing tonic of the senses."[8] *La Notte* depicts a study of moods between a husband (Marcello Mastroianni) and wife (Jeanne Moreau), two people who have lost all real ability to communicate with one another. The main part of the action is set at a party given by a rich industrialist, a setting typical of many contemporary films and a descendant of Renoir's *The Rules of the Game.*

At this party the wife, Lidia, becomes involved with a young man; the husband, Giovanni, with the daughter of the host. As in Fellini's *La Dolce Vita,* we are pilgrims on a dusk-to-dawn journey of illusions and disillusions, of enchantments and disenchantments. In the gray morning light, Lidia and Giovanni wander through the millionaire's golf course. Calmly, she tells him he is a writer for whom words have substituted for life. Feeling no love for him, she is helpless to separate. Uneasy and perplexed, Giovanni begins to make passionate love to his wife at the edge of a sand trap. "But I don't love you any more," she says. "Be quiet," he mutters as he continues his automated sexual overture.

In Antonioni's films we even see the soulless, degenerate eroticism mirrored in the landscape—desolate, with wide streets, open plazas, vacant lots, neglected buildings, and antiseptic modern structures. The dreary spiritual attitudes of despair and weariness are as monotonously modular as the material artifacts of skyscrapers, high-rise apartments, and manorial residences. Antonioni seems to be asking: Is the modern Western world becoming a mausoleum, shining and polished on the exterior, but inside full of dead man's bones? If forms of lovemaking within Western marriages are as revelatory as Antonioni suggests, then is not our civilization really a whited sepulchre?

The crux of the problem of sex lies in *La Notte.* What is it that is neither reached nor communicated by sexual union as represented in this film? Why does Lidia no longer feel for Giovanni? Solovyev has written some very trenchant lines on the basic abnormality of merely satisfying so-called biologically natural needs.[9] If sexual behavior as studied legally, medically, and psychoanalytically is based on the assumption of some dislocation in "normal sexual relationships" such as fetishism, where some part (e.g., a woman's silk stocking) is the object of a love that should be directed to the entire person, why, asks Solovyev, is this more unnatural than the limitation of sex fulfillment to just physical union between male and female? Solovyev concludes that the studies on *psycopathia sexualis* are based on vague, fortuitous, and arbitrary norms of sexual relationships. The basis seems to be only that of statistical frequency, in short its social acceptance through "use and custom."[10]

What, then, of the sex revolution as mirrored by the international cinema? Jean Renoir captured the significance of Solovyev's thesis in his short film, *A Day in the Country*. Adapted from a Guy de Maupassant story, the film recounts an outing on the banks of the Marne of a merchant, his wife, and their daughter. Both mother and daughter are seduced: the former not only acquiesces but, indeed, cooperates; the latter submits as a wounded, tremulous animal about to die. Can we speak of seduction in both cases? Is not the daughter's case closer to moral rape? Is not the mother an accomplice since, after all, the intention, the knowledge, the spontaneity of will are the decisive factors in sexual union?

Where, then, does society's definitions of morality and normality stop and immorality and perversion begin? The controversial film of Basil Dearden, *Victim*, is a relevant example. A wage clerk is apprehended for stealing money from a construction firm to pay those who blackmailed him for being a homosexual. Like *Tea and Sympathy*, *Victim* treats inversion not as a secondary theme, but as the main plot. It is a message movie, purposely designed to modify the British legal penalties on homosexuality. Following the suicide of the blackmailed clerk in a prison cell, a noted barrister (Dirk Bogarde), takes the case to heart, largely because he has mastered his earlier homosexual leanings to lead a "normal" married life. Intent on identifying the blackmailers, the lawyer comes upon homosexuals in every stratum of society who are being victimized by a combination of antiquated statutes and ruthless extortionists. One is reminded of the blackmail of a Senator in Otto Preminger's *Advice and Consent* and *Time*'s comment: "Nowhere does the film suggest that homosexuality is a serious (but often curable) neurosis that attacks the biological basis of life itself.[11] In a protest much less eloquent and convincing than that of M when captured by the underworld, one homosexual victim says: "I can't help the way I am. Nature played me a dirty trick." Once transcendence in society becomes foreshortened through a truncated concept of man's spiritual reach, there is no end to the broadening of the varieties of sexual experience. At that point, nature can logically be expected to shoulder all responsibility for psychiatric and medical problems in the domain of sexual activity. *Victim* is a dramatic instance of such psychic determinism.

This trend is growing, in part due to the new "X" classification for "adult" films and in part due to the changing mores of a world-wide urban industrialization trend. Marcuse believes that a repressive desublimation is taking place, namely the "release of sexuality in modes and forms which reduce and weaken erotic energy," enabling the Reality Principle to extend its hold over Eros.[12] Something like this seems to be happening, although it is never easy to measure the role of a medium such as motion pictures in such a process. There seems to be some sociomoral principle of Heisenberg at work so that films speed up social causation, thus effecting people subjectively in unascertainable ways. At the same time it performs an objective role, reflecting the concrete events and processes of social history. More research is needed on film in its dual role of being simultaneously an index of an objective world and an agent that shapes the consciousness of subjects in that same world. Perhaps a few remarks on a cinematic sexual theology would serve as a preface to such a study.

What are the unexamined assumptions of the majority of films that deal with sex, especially those of the underground cinema? Are they not, as Solovyev indicated, designed to shock the middle class values of society? Whereas once we were shocked by *Gone With the Wind*, when Clark Gable's Rhett Butler told Vivien Leigh's Scarlett O'Hara "I don't give a damn," today the shadow language of the street manifests itself in all the bright light of the silver screen so that in *The Killing of Sister George*, the protagonist clearly mouthes a barrack expletive that even hardened soldiers refrain from uttering in polite society. Is graffiti becoming part of screenplay dialogue? The danger in employing statistical frequency as the norm for typical behavior is that such behavior can be changed, and with it the definition of normality. This can be seen in Antonioni's *La Notte*, where we are confronted with sexual pathology in the deepest Solovyevian sense. "Sexual absolutizing" is as grievous for man's spirit as the "absolutizing of sex." The challenge to the international cinema in the 1970s will be to strike a balance sex between a puritanical extreme and that of pathology as defined by Solovyev. Today many movieviewers are tempted to utter the

Shakespearian curse "on both your houses" regarding the absolutizing of sex, such as in the New York State Board of Censors' ban on Jeff Musso's perceptive film, *The Puritan*, and the sexual absolutizing syndrome evident in films such as *I Am Curious (Yellow)*, *I, a Woman*, and *Dear John*.

The challenge to motion pictures becomes particularly evident in a spate of films on inversion and perversion: *The Boys in the Band*, *The Servant*, *Reflections in a Golden Eye*, *The Sergeant*, *Midnight Cowboy*, *The Killing of Sister George*, *Thérèse and Isabelle*, *The Fox*, *The Collector*, *The Detective*, *The Staircase*, *Secret Ceremony*, and *The Queen*, to name some of the prominent English-speaking pictures of the past decade on sodomy, lesbianism, and transvestism. One could easily add to this list such foreign items as *Fellini Satyricon*, *The Damned*, and *Belle du Jour*.

It is hard to underestimate the influence of Freud and the neo-Freudian tradition on films. Not only have Westerns been affected in recent years by considerations of depth psychology (e.g., *The Left-Handed Gun*, *The Last Sunset*, and *The Hanging Tree*), but the erotic film has been affected as well. Martha Wolfenstein and Nathan Leites have taken films not as an "economic-entertainment" hybrid but as psychologic field material in their book, *Movies: A Psychologic Study*.[13] They show how often in the same female character are fused the tendencies of a siren and of a mother, illuminating Freud's observation that Western man's dilemma consists in satisfying in a single woman companion the dual requirement of a mistress and a mother. Since this study, the Freudian hypothesis has been expanded so as to cast the psychological ambiguity of "good" (i.e., angelic) and "bad" (i.e., carnal) to other relations of inversion, perversion, and reversion. Films which serve sheer statistical popularity in sexual matters tend to foreshorten the transcendental reach between the sexes. In the case of Bergman's somber trilogy, *Through a Glass Darkly*, *Winterlight*, and *Silence*, this redirection of sexual transcendence into channels of incest, sacrilege, and masturbation respectively is not necessarily an alienating experience from God. One is reminded of Graham Greene's trilogy, *The Power and the Glory*, *Brighton Rock*, and *The Heart of the Matter* (all later creditable motion pictures). In those films the existential fact of helplessness or hardness before one's own sexual and other debilities is the measure of divine compassion. (Pinky in *Brighton Rock* seems the only one doomed.) As significant as the final state of damnation that an author like Greene may foreordain for his character is the general indifference of countless people who no longer search to regain the "divine scent" of transcedence.

The basic question is not the culpability of the persons caught between inner psychic drives and outer social restraints. Here movieviewers tend to be sympathetic, even prone to excuse sexual deviance. On the other hand, moralists, religious educators, and, in general, the guardians of youth and community values are sensitive to "the pitfalls of sexual passion." As an industry first and an art form secondly, the motion picture gravitates more toward the tastes of the mass public than that of the elite "gatekeepers" of the religious and moral heritage of a society. The magnetic lines of economic force cannot be overlooked in trying to assess film's role as a mirror or a molder of a sexual ethos. This book inclines to the proposition that the motion picture has been a shaper of sexual mores rather than a mirror reflecting such habits.

The film *The Mark* may focus our discussion on this point. It concerns a man convicted for molesting small girls (in the actual case on which it was based, the crime was rape). Starring Mark Whitman as the traumatized man, Maria Schell as a widow with a pre-teenage daughter, and Rod Steiger as the psychiatrist, *The Mark* charts the struggle of the protagonist back to a life of adult heterosexuality. Unlike *The Victim*, this film does not insinuate any deterministic patterns of behavior that are beyond cure by the aid of medicine, psychoanalysis, religion, and understanding affection. If *The Mark* is too pat with its happy ending (the widow and the ex-convict in one another's arms), notwithstanding, the film's direction is theologically sound, if not artistically and clinically convincing.

The lesson of *The Mark* that love is superb therapy was lacking in *The Victim*. When Maria Schell entrusts her daughter to the psychoanalytic patient, knowing full well his clinical and criminal record, it is a sign of trust of the highest order. There can be no adequate discussion of sexual love as a major moment in the process of human transcendence without the treatment of altruism, the bond of selflessness that is the hyphen in any "I–Thou" relationship.

Let us look at the same principle but in its negative applications. Juan Bardem's *The Love-Maker* shows how repugnant it is to use people for selfish ends. Betsy Blair plays an unattractive girl over thirty who is made the object of a pool-hall bet. José Suárez, as one of the pool-hall crowd, accepts a wager whereby he is to feign love for the homely spinster. As in *Bonnie and Clyde*, what begins as a lark turns to tragedy as the lad, realizing the seriousness of the situation, is too weak to head off the girl's disillusionment. The final scene, intense in its display of injustice and embarrassment, succeeds in identifying the audience with the girl, who, prepared to turn an "I–Thou" relationship into a "We" situation, finds suddenly that she was "It." Seldom has the cinema caught such pain, furnishing the most persuasive psychological arguments for Solovyev's theory of love. For it is Solovyev who maintains that contrary to nature are not only the sex practices listed by a Marquis de Sade, a Krafft-Ebing, or a Henry Miller, but also whatever smacks of being a "deficiency of the higher spiritual consecration and satisfaction of emotional needs after the fashion of the lower animals."[14] The primacy of giving in a self-effacing, spontaneous manner is the essence of love, even sexual love.

A splendid example of this is William Gibson's play *Two for the Seesaw*, made into a motion picture with Robert Mitchum and Shirley MacLaine as the pair of lonely, confused people in New York who fall in love. Jerry is an Omaha lawyer who flees his possessive wife, a wealthy woman who can buy a career for her mate. Gittel Mosca is a Bronx-bred Jewish girl, hardened by experience. While she is an ambitious ballet dancer, she is plagued with an ulcer. Their dialogue is comical and their habits casual. They have a love affair, but deep down they know it cannot go on. Jerry has standards; Gittel is unprepossessing in her goodhearted concern for Jerry. She will allow him to return to his wife in Omaha. In this picture the towering skyline is not the symbol of man's pride, which Antonioni used at the outset of *La Notte* as the start of his descent into the hell of an empty marriage. Rather, it counterpoints the anonymity of a city, where loneliness can not long remain unmitigated by some relief. The erotic is transient and secondary

in both play and movie as it was in *Dr. Zhivago*. The appearance of Robert Mitchum recalls his role in *Heaven Knows, Mr. Allison*, where two characters, basically noble, also learn some enduring truths about themselves. Finally, *Two for the Seesaw* is redolent of the plot of *A Taste of Honey*, a brief respite through love from the weary life on this checkerboard of days and nights.

Two for the Seesaw is shot through with some profound psychological insights on sacrifice as the deepest expression of total human love. The spare telephone dialogue of the final separation between Jerry and Gittel, bright with "Bronxisms," is a profound theological gloss on the timeless essence of human love:

GITTEL: You been a great help, Jerry, it's the first affair I—I come out with more than I went in. I mean, wherever this guy is, he'll owe you!

JERRY: (*a pause, humbly*) Thank you for that. And she'll owe you more than she'll know. After—(*he tries to recall it*) After the verb to love, to help is

GITTEL: (*a pause*) What, Jerry?

JERRY: The sweetest in the tongue. Somebody said it. We. . . . (*He looks at his watch.*) Well, so long, infant, (*Gittel tries to say it, but her eyes are full, her heart is in her mouth, and she struggles to keep it from overflowing there; she cannot.*)

GITTEL: I love you, Jerry! (*Jerry is rigid; it takes her a moment to go on.*) Long as you *live* I want you to remember the last thing you heard out of me was I love you!

JERRY: (*long pause*) "I love you too, Gittel." (*He hangs up, and for a moment there is no movement*).

This is not Freudian dialogue, where sublimation is mere release of sexual tension only through nonerotic channels; it is much more. It is sacrifice: the enrichment of one life by another and thereby elevated to a nonsexual plane of union. In his excellent book, *The Art of Loving*, Erich Fromm quotes Karl Marx on the regenerative powers of genuine love not only for the beloved but the loving partner as well. In 1884, Marx wrote: "When you love but are not loved reciprocally, that is, when your loving does not find any return, when your affirmations of being a loving person do not cause you to be beloved, then is your love powerless, a sorry thing.[15] The test of love, therefore, is not one of accepted usage, nor a physiological one of pleasure maximization, nor a psychological one of blind inevitability. Rather, the test of all love, especially sexual, is in terms of total giving on the psychological and spiritual levels as well as on the biological and physiological ones.

Six principles can be derived from this discussion of a cinematic sexual theology.

1. Sexual union is never a negative mode of transcendence except when the transcendental aspect of reciprocal surrender is contradicted either in the act itself (i.e., *La Notte*) or by a lack of sustained fidelity in the nonerotic areas of the love relationship (*This Sporting Life*). The autonomy of the sexual act, even when graced by reciprocal surrender (*Hiroshima, Mon Amour, Dr. Zhivago*), begs a complementary social and sacramental seal to perfect the divinization of love about which Solovyev has so eloquently written.

2. Virginity or the renouncement of sexual union, if graced by true surrender to God, is not a deficient mode of human love (*Heaven Knows, Mr. Allison*). Moreover, celibate love, while enjoying the same autonomy as sexual love, does not necessarily need any peculiar complementary sign to advertise its divine reference (*Monsieur Vincent*). True there are the religious vow and the sacrament of priesthood that, in the case of Roman Catholics, still signify a spiritual renouncement of a sublime earthly right.

3. The transcendental complement to sexual union, insists Solovyev in *The Meaning of Love*, is found beyond biological union and earthly morality in a bond of spiritual life, in which the majority of intelligent people either do not believe or allow only in poetry.[16] Ingmar Bergman is the great film chronicler of the forms of bourgeois love and the efforts to gain transcendence by departures from earthly morality. The later chapter on death shall try to link his attraction for this theme with his search for more than grudging resignation regarding mature love beyond the stages of tender love and erotic gaming. Antonioni has expressed a similar brand of fatalism concerning love in Western secular civilization (*L'Avventura, La Notte*), more bitter and despairing than Jean Renoir's chipping away of the thin social veneer that covers the baser instincts of such proper people as in *The Rules of the Game* and *A Day in the Country*.

4. While liberty is an essential ingredient of sexual relationships,

the combination of puritanical pressures, personal passions, and the contemporary spirit of competition and acquisitiveness have all conspired to reduce man's free response to the transcendental demands of love. The insights of Freud and Marx, implicit in many motion pictures, explain the growing elasticity of sexual mores together with a progressive rationalization of other aspects of life. The result is gained at the expense of economic and political freedom and greater sexual indulgence, as Marcuse maintains in *Eros and Civilization*. One could add to Marcuse's thesis that a true psychological liberty is lost (e.g., *Victim*) that can only be gained not by relaxed laws, as desirable and necessary as this is at times, but by moral effort along the transcendental axis (*The Mark*). The growing popularity of films on inversion and perversion is more than a sign of greater tolerance; it is a confirmation of Marcuse's prediction that the rationalization of man and society leads to a libidinal morality, a new ethos of legitimized gratification.[17]

5. The use of another person as an instrument of gratification (e.g., *The Love-Maker*), implied in every libidinal morality, is repugnant not only to the Judaeo-Christian premises of Western civilization but also to all the great Eastern religions such as Buddhism, Hinduism, and Confucianism.

6. The "I–Thou" relation of Martin Buber, so innate an element of reciprocal affection both in sexual union and platonic friendship, is not predicated only on physical intimacy and presence alone but also on such sacrifices as separation and renunciation as the welfare of the other requires it (e.g., *Heaven Knows, Mr. Allison, Dr. Zhivago*, and *A Taste of Honey*). The entire spiritualization process can be summed up in the words: "To love is to help" (*Two for the Seesaw*).

Courtesy: United Artists Corporation.

Humphrey Bogart in *Maltese Falcon*.

6

A Cinematic Theology of Evil

JOSEPH LOSEY'S *The Servant* gives us perhaps the most vivid account of deliberate evil ever presented on the screen. The unraveling of the moral fiber of a young English aristocrat, Tony (James Fox), is gradual, starting slowly with his growing dependence on a mild-looking butler, Barrett (Dirk Bogarde), who serves as a jack-of-all-trades. Losey depicts three clear stages of descent into the morass of evil. First is the affair Tony has with Vera (Sarah Miles), whom Barrett has brought to the house as his sister; she is actually his fiancée. Trapped in this compromising situation, Tony is taken with his servant's unruffled manners that ingratiate him progressively into the confidence of his master, and beyond that into a homosexual relationship; from there it is only a short step to marijuana and hard drugs. The plot has all the classic lines of the old nineteenth-century print of "The Rake's Progress," with the gradual descent and then rapid disintegration of a person. Losey's film is a manual of evil, only surpassed by *The Exorcist*.

However, theology must seek to enlarge the focus of evil beyond that presented in the personalized forms of evil such as Barrett, who reminds us of Mephistopheles in *Faust* (e.g., Richard Burton's role as Faust) or Iago taunting the credulous Moor (dramatized by both Orson Welles and Laurence Olivier in their film versions of *Othello*). Like the fickle subatomic particles of nuclear physics, evil sometimes acts like a "wave" reaching out in all directions in formless ways; suddenly it begins to act as an identifiable mass of concentrated malice with clearly defined boundaries that we can give names to, such as Barrett, Mephistopheles, or Iago. Speaking of incarnate forms of evil, several films have touched the question of witchcraft: *Black Orpheus*, *The Crucible*, *Day of Wrath*, and *Rosemary's Baby*. While all religions refer to some force of evil, often even personalizing it, this study, rather than dealing with diabolic phenomena such as witchcraft, will discuss the more amorphous and less visible kinds of evil.

The patterns of diffusion regarding evil are manifold and difficult to diagnose. St. Augustine tried to track evil down to its very source only to become lost in fogs of mystery. Without pretending to be able to uncover the origins of evil, I hope to sharpen the questions regarding evil and its spread through cinema case studies.

Evil is a multicephalous hydra capable of reproducing heads as fast as they are cut off. This seems to be the lesson Elia Kazan wished to convey in his film of Budd Schulberg's screenplay, *A Face in the Crowd*. Like Robert Aldrich's *The Big Knife*, the title of Kazan-Schulberg's film is thought-provoking—almost meditative— for it links the personal ("face") with the impersonal ("crowd"). The film begins with a radio program in northwest Arkansas called "A Face in the Crowd." The female interviewer, Marcia (Patricia Neal), asks a local prison inmate, Lonesome Rhodes (Andy Griffith), to sing for her listeners. Having been charged with drunkenness and vagrancy, he is pardoned through Marcia's intervention, obtains a job with the radio station and begins to gain a reputation as an entertainer. Together with the crescendo of fame comes the simultaneous decrescendo of character. The plot moves within three cities, signifying steps on the ladder of Rhodes's ascent to fame. In Pickett, Arkansas, Lonesome and Marcia become close. In Memphis, as a television celebrity, he becomes self-assured, acquires a promoter, Joey de Palma, and seduces Marcia. Finally he is brought to New York, where he first attracts a sponsor whose chief representative is a former career officer, General Haynesworth. Soon he gains 65 million viewers and very high audience ratings. Haynesworth introduces him to a Senator Fuller who wants to make him President. He is now at the pinnacle of success that he shares with an old road companion, Beanie, with whom he has been reunited. He proposes to Marcia, feeling that he needs her support.

Having been married earlier, Lonesome stops in Pickett, Arkansas, on his way to Mexico for a divorce. The townspeople hold a reception for their favorite singer whom they launched to fortune and glory. Also present is a young blonde majorette, Betty Lou (Lee Remick), whom, as Marcia later discovers, Lonesome marries. He returns to New York and becomes involved with Senator Fuller. The dénouement comes when Lonesome caustically speaks out his mind, not knowing that he is on the air. This leads to his downfall, and he becomes a social pariah repudiated by the media, his sponsors, the account executives of the advertising agency, his audience, and his political contacts. No longer does he hobnob with the power elite. Nor is he any longer, as Schulberg described him, "a man who takes it for granted that he will be agreed with and that there is no subject he cannot master."[7] The film ends with Marcia leaving by taxi while above we see and hear Lonesome on his New York penthouse balcony, repeating in a rasping, broken voice: "Marcia, don't leave me. . . . Don't leave me. . . . Don't leave. . . ." As in *The Servant*, Lonesome is another broken man, but this time one who is corrupted by the strange alchemy of "a way of life" that, as Schulberg has said in another context, "was paying dividends in the first half of the twentieth century."[2]

Whereas in *The Servant* the focuses of evil are two, Barrett and Vera, in *A Face in the Crowd* they are numerous. Marcia commits the indiscretion of going into a prison for program material for her radio audience, patronizing the prisoners on behalf of utilitarian ends; Joey de Palma is the hustling promoter who exploits the talents of others (reminiscent of Schulberg's Sammy Glick in *What Makes Sammy Run?*); Mel Miller, the television program producer in Nashville, whose intellectual perceptions see through the economic system that those same talents strengthen. Betty Lou is the brainless blonde who trades on her beauty and lives without much thought for the future, for others, or even for the consequences of her actions and inactions; General Haynesworth is the ex-military officer now turned executive, who believes in Lonesome Rhodes's political value as a symbol for the nation, since "in every strong and healthy society from the Egyptians to our own, the mass had to be guided with a strong hand by a responsible elite"; Senator Fuller, an aging member of the great body of the upper House, who dis-

Photograph courtesy of Walter Reade 16.

Akira Kurosawa's *High and Low*.

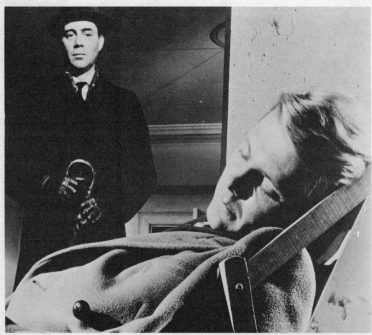

Courtesy: Commonwealth United Entertainment, Inc.

Dirk Bogarde in *The Servant*.

simulates his real intentions because he knows what's best for the American people better than they; and Beanie, Lonesome's old crony from pre-fame days, who is beyond evil just as Lonesome himself is, because of his uncritical acceptance of what is. Lonesome Rhodes is preyed upon by all these people as much as Tony is by Barrett in *The Servant*. The archvillain in the movie is not television, although no other film has centered on its mesmerizing powers as much as this one (not even *Medium Cool*, which handled the political impact of live television news coverage). The archvillain, if we must point to one, is the public; the passive, consumeristic television-viewing public whose sleeping instincts can be suddenly and terrifyingly awakened and shaped into a colossal singleminded millipede led by a Lonesome Rhodes with his guitar, his folk songs, "chatty" patter, and a 48.7 Trendex rating. The demagogic possibilities, frightening in their prospects, are also developed in *Expresso Bongo*, *The Great Man*, *Loving You*, *Your Cheatin' Heart*, and *Wild in the Streets*.

This reality of evil is close to those who work in and for institutions. They are so close to it that they find it hard to detach themselves from it and to relate to it. Consequently, religious sermons, catechism classes, and pronouncements by church leaders seem aloof to many people. They seek a more existential theology of evil, one that connects the many strands of cause and effect into the giant web of man's complicity in what Paul of Tarsus called "the mystery of iniquity." An urgent task before us is to relate the evil of individual violence to the larger pattern of institutional violence so that crimes of passion, frustration, and resentment are seen as interconnected with socially permissible deeds of collusion, market manipulations, and opportunistic self-enrichment devices such as lobbying and legal loopholes. The poignant ending of Kurosawa's *High and Low* brings both these worlds together in a brilliant kaleidoscopic fusion. André Cayatte undertook something similar in his brace of films, *My Nights with Françoise* and *My Days with André Marc*, in which the same story was repeated to give both the man's and the woman's viewpoint. Any world-embracing religious creed must teach us to beware of subliminal complicity in serving systems that promote evil.

The world of evil presented by motion pictures has progressively tended to fuse the "black-and-white" moral judgments into a grayish picture of society. The American cinema of the thirties was the classic period of spectacular gunmen, hoodlums, and public enemies, that is, evil personified with no reference to social causation. Later in the forties and fifties came a more sophisticated view of the criminal than that portrayed by George Raft, Paul Muni, Edward G. Robinson, James Cagney, and Humphrey Bogart. The criminal type is not a social leper, cruel and feared. He is coming closer to the "half-and-half" hero cited earlier, the badman who believes himself no worse than the society that pursues him: Alan Ladd (*This Gun for Hire*), Tyrone Power (*Johnny Apollo*), John Garfield (*The Postman Always Rings Twice*), Tony Curtis (*Six Bridges to Cross*), and John Cassavetes (*Crime in the Streets*), to mention a few sympathetic criminal types. The theological implications of such twilight characters furnish a synoptic view of person and society, thus minimizing whatever determinism exists in blind surrender to social forces. As society became more interdependent in its specialization of tasks, films naturally began to accept the formal artistry of the robber and the gunman in an amoral way as a fact of life performed with distinction. Jules Dassin's *Rififi* and *Topkapi* looked at crime through such lenses, as did *The Godfather*.

This general temper of moral neutrality has reached its height in what is called the "now" movie. Such films, like so many music, dance, and art forms in the 1960s, have little regard for the audience in terms of ready comprehension or enjoyment. They are introverted, highly personal statements, not infrequently an *apologia pro vita sua* for misfits, neurotics, and socially marginal types. One thinks of the offbeat pathological female liar in Richard Lester's *Petulia*, and the action for action's sake in his *A Hard Day's Night*, *Help!*, and *The Knack. . . . and how to get it;* the schizoid nonconformist in Karl Reisz's *Morgan!;* the confused, oversize adolescent in Silvio Narizzano's *Georgy Girl;* the nihilistic females in Godard's *La Chinoise* and *Vivre sa Vie;* the naive female and male sex pets of John Schlesinger's *Darling* and *Midnight Cowboy*.

This is all to say that if film is a fair barometer of social trends, then recent trends show evil to be more a wave phenomenon (diffuse as in the "half-and-half" hero) than a particle phenomenon (in the form of a Mephistopheles or a Iago). Films are valuable heuristic devices for showing the ability of evil to don different masks, as Lon Chaney did in the silent era of cinema.

Since evil is diffuse, we are all accomplices to some greater or lesser degree in its generation, maintenance, and propagation. This may seem startling until one reflects on how many of us little realize that, by laughing at a Charlie Chaplin or a Jacques Tati, we are really laughing at our own foibles. Similarly, we often lack the ironic sensibility to appreciate starker films such as *The Incident, The Graduate, Goodbye, Columbus,* and *Easy Rider,* not completely aware that the characters whom we recognize as weak, unheroic, and conforming are basically only types of ourselves. One of the most sardonic psychological phenomena in this regard took place with the role of the Common Man in the stage version of Robert Bolt's *A Man for All Seasons.* Petty, opportunistic, and cautious, the Common Man throughout the play takes care of himself in an obvious, calculating way. Albert Dekker, who played the Duke of Norfolk on Broadway, once said that although it was obvious that Bolt intended the audience to recognize themselves in the Common Man's actions and attitudes, they identified invariably with St. Thomas More. We are accomplices. In a certain sense, as a French film once suggested, we are all murderers—if not in deed or intent, then by our complicity through deeds of omission.

While admission of complicity is invariably difficult, irony should not be difficult for persons with true religious sensibilities. It is a sense of irony which is the key to a more profound understanding of the various forms of military, political, religious, and economic evil. And, indeed, cinema can help to broaden one's understanding of how institutions serve as capillaries for the propagation of evil. One fine instance of military complicity in evil is found in James Jones's World War II novel, *The Thin Red Line,* later filmed by Andrew Marton. A good example of the transformation that military life under battle conditions can wreak on normal, even shy, men, the movie casts considerable light, for instance, on the psychology of the American soldiers involved in the slaying of 109 Vietnamese civilians at My Lai in March 1968.[3]

The Thin Red Line is set on a South Pacific island infested by Japanese. The sergeant (Jack Warden) is typically hard-crusted, a martinet who has two objectives uppermost in mind, progress against the enemy and the safety of his men. These ends, mutually exclusive, are the nub of the plot. The sensitive private (Keir Dullea) is not a killer, but in order to survive he must kill. When he is wounded and sees the enemy sniper advancing with a bayonet, he reacts like a cornered tiger and chokes the Japanese to death. This killing serves the sergeant's first goal as well as the second. The film takes a psychological turn as the sergeant flouts his underling with the accusation that he likes to kill. Each killing lowers the barrier of inhibition, while, paradoxically, the private is reluctant to admit that he and the sergeant are of the same stripe, professional killers fighting under the greatest rationalization man has conjured up— patriotism. The final scene, when Dullea goes into a killing frenzy with a machinegun, is one of the most convincing indictments of war. It would be interesting to compare such American films with Masaki Kobayashi's powerful antiwar film about the Manchurian war, *The Human Condition*, or other military pictures such as *Paths of Glory, From Here to Eternity, Attack*, and *M*A*S*H**.

How do we theologically evaluate such films? Basically we use the same method of nonpreconception applied earlier to *A Face in the Crowd*. In both films conscience is but one face of the coin of reality, of which the other is society. In *A Face in the Crowd* we saw both the compounding of personal weakness and the escalation of absurdity in the communications subculture. As in that film, in *The Thin Red Line* there is also no single villain, just a hellbroth of extenuating circumstances and cross-purposes boiling over onto well-meaning, sometimes weak, persons. Some are "true believers" such as the sergeant, who has given himself over unreflectingly to the military bureaucracy. Then there are the "half believers," such as the private, who only has one fundamental negative conviction, that a mad society has no right to tax his credulity or life to the utmost. He clings to life and in so doing becomes skeptical. After all, what is left for anyone trying to keep out of the slough of brutality that war represents? Why does there seem to be so much gratuitous, unnecessary evil? Why must there be peacetime standing armies whose spiritual price is rarely discussed: the danger of loneliness and temptation to homosexuality (John Huston's *Reflections in a Golden Eye*), the inclination to sadism and excessive authoritarianism (Fred Zinneman's *From Here to Eternity*), barracks boredom (Jack Gold's *The Bofors Gun*), and the vice career-ism and goldbricking (John Boulting's *Private Progress*).

As for the web of evil in which politics is enmeshed among several fine studies (e.g., *Advise and Consent, The Last Hurrah, Wild in the Streets,* and *Tennessee Johnson*), one film stands out: Robert Rossen's *All The King's Men,* a screen version of Robert Penn Warren's prize-winning fictitious account of Huey Long. Set in Louisiana, we see how a red-necked, country farmer becomes a ruthless demagogue. As most immoral men who arrive at a position of power, he learns to surround himself with both brawn and brains. American politics is witnessing a recrudescence of the southern political boss so well described in Rossen's film: the strong-willed, honey-tongued governor who mastered the Machiavellian art of dissimulating his real designs. The case of Huey Long, closed by bullets a third of a century ago, is a textbook study of corruption. In *All the King's Men,* Broderick Crawford earned an Oscar playing the lead role of a megalomaniac who, stopping at nothing to retain power, blackmails a state judge. The film is a geometrical proof of Lord Acton's famous dictum that power tends to corrupt and abso-lute power tends to corrupt absolutely. Here again we have the "true believer," who has fixed ideas that appeal to the masses for their simplicity and conviction.

Religious studies of evil are found in the coarse-grained examples (e.g., the ecclesiastical judges in *The Passion of Joan of Arc*) and the more refined case studies (e.g., the Mother Superior in *A Nun's Story*). There is a common temptation to focus on individual vil-lains in situations of total institutionalization such as a barracks, a convent, or a school. But these individuals are often only the reflec-tions of larger social systems that bestow authority on them. This is very evident in Raymond Rouleau's film, *The Crucible,* adapted in France by Jean-Paul Sartre from Arthur Miller's play. The play is intended as a direct attack on the paranoiac campaign of Senator Joseph McCarthy against communism and its sympathizers, and it takes the form of the seventeenth-century witch trials in Salem, Massachusetts. The film was made in France since Miller was black-listed in the United States.

Set in Salem in 1692, the film features Yves Montand as John Proctor, a Puritan farmer, and his wife Elizabeth, played by Simone

Signoret. Elizabeth surprises her husband with a servant, Abigail, and eventually sends the girl away. Abigail, resentful, organizes a group of young girls to assist her in some seances in the forest. Caught by the pastor, Abigail pleads as her defense that she is a sorceress. Everyone is in state of suspense about the matter. The Governor of the Province comes and sets up a court of inquiry. But the pastor's reasonable arguments fall on the deaf ears of his parishioners, backed by the richest farmers. The witch-hunts begin and denunciations multiply. When Abigail accuses Elizabeth and has her arrested, John confesses to his affair with Abigail, thus unmasking her motives for accusing Elizabeth. However, when Elizabeth refuses to denounce her husband as an adulterer, he too is sentenced. While Elizabeth, pregnant, has her death sentence commuted, John and two others are hung in the prison courtyard while a crowd rages outside to prevent it. The film ends with a funeral procession and the insistence of Elizabeth that Abigail not be lynched.

The Crucible makes an important point, namely, the psychoanalytic connection between puritanical attitudes and political reactionary movements. The hippies may exaggerate this thesis when they recommend us to "Make love, not war." Nevertheless, clinical psychology has shown that certain types of nonrepressive therapy do release pent-up forces of aggressiveness and hate. In *The Crucible*, the diffusion of evil in the Salem witchcraft trials is a consequence of the workings of the subconscious that psychiatric and medical research have uncovered only in the past hundred years. Believing that racial hatred, social tension, political crusades, and religious fanaticism are outcroppings of deep sexual dislocations, Arthur Miller also stressed this nexus in *Focus* and in *A View from the Bridge*. One need not subscribe to any neo-Freudian viewpoint to be aware of subterranean psychic forces that account in large measure for religious intolerance and persecution.

In the matter of the diffusion of evil in business and labor, there are some excellent film studies, such as *Patterns*, *On the Waterfront*, *The Angry Silence*, and *Executive Suite*. A particularly interesting one is Alexander Mackendrick's *The Man in the White Suit*.[4] As a farce, this film provides an excellent vehicle for probing evil in business, perhaps better than any *film noir* on the subject.

This is because a tongue-in-cheek approach to vested interests is possibly the best way filmmakers can critically treat ticklish problems that could cause economic backlash. The British are eminently successful at this type of social satire, generally as piquantly funny as it is instructive. Who can easily forget Peter Sellers's Anglican priest in *Heavens Above!*, and what a prophetic contrast he represented to the local ecclesiastical structure and its ties to the town's influential merchants and wealthy families. In the same category were the barbs hurled at the featherbedding tactics of unions in *I'm All Right, Jack*. One can make forthright social analyses if the rapier of criticism is blunted somewhat by the button-tip of humor. A film such as *I'm All Right, Jack* is much more revealing in the final analysis than the more somber *The Angry Silence*, just as *The Man in the White Suit* is more successful in its humorous way than Kurosawa's avowed exposure of corporate ethics and practices in *The Bad Sleep Well*.

Alec Guinness's role in *The Man in the White Suit* is that of an inventor, more speculative than practical, more trusting than strategic, more naive than worldly wise. He is a scientific Peter Pan who, in a world of carefully measured self-interests, carries with him, as an astronaut in the alien environment of space, his own supply of moral oxygen. Subtract his character out of the film together with certain humorous touches of the director and the film becomes asphyxiating.

The film's humorous assumption is that the inventor has found a material that neither wears out nor becomes dirty. Guinness's time-resistant and nonstainable white suit is a triumph of research and development that he understandably wishes to share with everyone, including his fellow workers and the management of the firm. However, his startling scientific discovery swiftly leads to an economic discovery, namely, how economic systems are motivated. He soon learns that his own methodology, based on linear, frictionless models of the laboratory, is quite distinct from the competitive dynamics of the marketplace. Both the union and management join forces to defeat an invention whose diffusion would be disastrous for an industry that rests on obsolescence. Time-perishable products make possible predictable sales forecasts, thus influencing capital investment, stimulating production, increasing employment, swelling labor's ranks and the union's coffers and providing the consumptive power that keeps a highly complex industrial system well-oiled. Guinness's scientific expertise had never grasped the economic interdependence of social systems and their delicate equilibrium.

As the picture ends, we discover that the material is not durable but comes apart like raw wool. Relieved, the once-threatened representatives of the union and the management enjoy the joke. However, the basic threat remains, for Guinness's eyes sparkle impishly in the final scene. He seems to be saying to himself: "Eureka—I have got it!" as he runs off to smooth out the flaw in his process to produce suits of immortal white. This thoroughly charming film is highly relevant for an existential theology of evil, for it captures brilliantly the thesis of Thorstein Veblen that while the machine age has changed much, the methods of businessmen have not changed fundamentally.[5] The same is valid for large-scale unionism which, in most developed nations of the West, forms an integral part of big business. This cinema case study shows the interlocking vicious circles that are difficult to sever.

In effect, we have returned to the theme of Robert Aldrich's *The Big Knife*. In all large structures where interdependence exists through delegated authority, specialization, and consensus mechanisms for decisions, there is a "big knife" with two blades: one amoral, used to cut an organizational path forward through the tangled jungle of the unknown future; and the other moral, to cut into the human spirit, challenging man to hallow the means to his own transcendent ends. The conflict is a classic one that we can recognize but not resolve. Awareness of the "big knife" dilemma does not separate good from evil: it merely makes man suffer the knowledge of good and evil in himself and all around him. In a world of larger and larger organizations, the "knives" are not only getting bigger and sharper, they are also being wielded with greater strength and rapidity.

There is a theological antinomy that arises out of the greater rationalization of life as foreseen by Max Weber, the German social historian. It consists in the transcendental achievements of ever-larger groups for mass government, mass production, mass defense, and mass religious services. As the "knives" grow, so does the alienation and feeling of helplessness of individuals within these organizations. Size is not intrinsically evil, argue some economists, management consultants, and corporation lawyers. Perhaps, but the artistic and biographical evidence is not convincing. Rod Serling, author of the television play about corporate ethics, *Patterns*, later made into a creditable film, once said that he received an astonishing number of fan letters after the original showing of this story.[6] Many believed the story was a fictitious account of a real corporation. Since the "big knife" dilemma is a perennial one, it is well to see it for what it is.

Take Orson Welles's pathbreaking *Citizen Kane*, a thinly disguised account of a wealthy publisher who established his newspaper syndicate not as much on competitive grounds of excellence or public preference as on the fact that he could invest his inherited millions to a degree his rivals could not. Has there ever been a picture of greater loneliness than the pinnacle of power attained by Kane? The evil that is diffused through an organization often has its center of gravity in the individual who guides it. Hollywood

Courtesy: United Artists Corporation.

Martha Raye and Charlie Chaplin in *Monsieur Verdoux*.

movies about Hollywood itself bring out this point quite effectively: *The Bad and the Beautiful, Sunset Boulevard, All About Eve, The Goddess, Inside Daisy Clover,* and *The Legend of Lylah Clare.* The industry that aims its camera down at the world from its Parnassian summit where dwell its celluloid gods and goddesses cannot help but receive reflected back the narcissistic gaze of this same camera. It is not surprising that Hollywood's corporate conscience is pricked now and again. Given man's transcendence, he has an insatiable curiosity to know—an urge similar to that of Oedipus—to want to trace the source of evil.

This same curiosity impelled Charlie Chaplin to make *Monsieur Verdoux,* a rich theological source for understanding the many masks of evil. Chaplin's Verdoux is an enemy of established society. As with the petty thief in *Pickpocket,* Verdoux has his own conscience that he esteems more rigorous, better calibrated, and socially more beneficial than the hypocritical codes of society. For Verdoux these codes feign righteousness but, in reality, breed war, hate, greed, and acquisitiveness. Consequently, Verdoux marries wealthy women who are, from his point of view, socially expendable. Having killed them one by one, he is apprehended, tried, found guilty, and sentenced to death. The final scene is full of irony. Although Verdoux sees the state as the agent of war, it presumes to pass judgment on him, a murderer of a few parasitical women, when it, the state, has perpetrated crimes that can only be calculated in megadeaths. His conscience is serene, since he sees his deeds as forms of poetic justice contrasted with what the world tolerates daily. He politely refuses the services of the chaplain on the grounds that his need for reconciliation is not with God but rather with man.

Admittedly, this has been but a surface analysis of evil. Any sustained research on this subject might profit from six basic conclusions reached here.

First, there is a personal incarnation of absolute evil as presented by both the literary and artistic imagination. This squares with the presence of a personal nonbiological fount of evil as found throughout diverse religious traditions that refer to Lucifer, Satan, Beelzebub, the Anti-Christ, the Evil One, the Father of Lies, and the devil. The question of persons in league with the devil are suggested by characters such as Mephistopheles (*Faust*), Iago (*Othello*), Barrett (*The Servant*), and the witches in Carl Dreyer's *Day of Wrath*, Raymond Rouleau's *The Crucible,* Roman Polanski's *Rosemary's Baby,* and William Friedkin's *The Exorcist.*

Secondly, evil is highly regenerative, given the necessary fertile soil. In Kazan's *A Face in the Crowd*, social systems become encrusted in evil attitudes, evil practices, and evil agents. The failure of mass media's ability in the United States to elevate mass tastes over time is an important datum for assessing Kazan's film of how the communications industry needs both theological insight and inspiration concerning the side effects it produces, often inadvertently. Just as no one lies gratuitously, so evil is never produced for evil's sake, especially in the case of large-scale organizations dedicated to providing a public service. The unconscious conspiracy of "downward resourcelessness" between public and media professionals is something that has been too little researched, theologically speaking. Other movies relevant to a cinematic theology of evil regarding the communications culture are: *A Hard Day's Night, Help!, Expresso Bongo, The Great Man, Loving You, Your Cheatin' Heart,* and *Putney Swope.*

Thirdly, crime films have become more ambiguous, psychologically showing both criminal (e.g., *This Gun for Hire*) and detective (e.g., *The Maltese Falcon*) to be "half-and-half" heroes. More and more it is the smoothness and style of the professional role that has become significant rather than the moral or social function (*The French Connection, Rififi, Topkapi, Bullitt, The Detective,* and *Harper*). The logical and theological consequences of the amoral secular man have issued in films of contemporary "kooks" (*Alfie, Georgy Girl, Morgan!, Petulia*). The characters in these films seem harmless, almost lovable. Still, one wonders if they are as neurotically irresponsible and innocuous as they are made to appear or whether they are not in some sense willing minions of evil.

Fourthly, man's complicity in evil is opaque to him for some mysterious reason, which psychiatry in its depth analyses of the subliminal have not yet thoroughly illuminated or commented upon. The mass audience tends, for example, to identify itself with the courageous, suffering hero rather than with the mediocre and opportunistic "side-line" characters of the plot (e.g., *A Man for All Seasons, The Court Martial of Billy Mitchell, A Nun's Story, Tennessee Johnson, The Man in the White Suit*). In these films we empathize with the hero, and rarely see ourselves as even tempted to persecute such noble types.

Fifthly, evil is organized not as evil but under names, titles, banners, and rubrics that stand for unobjectionable goals such as law and order, prosperity, security, and sanctity. Under the umbrella of these hallowed causes the bacteria of evil that cannot ordinarily live in sunlight thrive and multiply. Any film can serve as fertile ground for studying the subterranean courses of evil in respectable institutions and social structures. Some especially pertinent movies in this regard are: *The Thin Red Line, The Human Condition, Paths of Glory, From Here to Eternity, Attack, Advise and Consent, The Last Hurrah, All the King's Men, Wild in the Streets, The Passion of Joan of Arc, The Crucible, Heavens Above!, I'm All Right, Jack, The Angry Silence, On the Waterfront, The Man in the White Suit, The Bad Sleep Well, Patterns,* and *Executive Suite.*

Sixthly, wherever transcendence is thwarted by systems unconscious of their complicity in evil, there follows a psychological backlash in terms of alienation, indifference, resignation, and a growing love-hate relationship toward the system. The first victim is the person within the system, such as the intelligence agent in *The Spy Who Came in From the Cold* and the tycoon in *Citizen Kane.* Many Hollywood exposé films trace this backlash pattern: *The Bad and the Beautiful, Sunset Boulevard, All About Eve, The Goddess, Inside Daisy Clover, The Oscar,* and *The Legend of Lylah Clare.* As did *The Big Knife,* these films reveal three interlocking circles: one of personal conscience, another of institutional mindlessness, and a third of some spiritual resolve either for or away from transcendence. If there is one thing a cinematic theology seems to deduce it is that there are metahistorical laws binding on all peoples, laws that man does not break so much as they break him. In this regard, one recalls what Hamlet called "a providence which shapes our ends, rough-hew them how we will." Kismet, Dharma, Fate, Clotho, Necessity—the names are as varied as those

Akira Kurosawa's *Ikiru* (To Live). Produced by Toho Co. Ltd. and distributed by Brandon Films, Inc.

Elizabeth Taylor and Richard Burton in *Who's Afraid of Virginia Woolf*.

describing evil, but evil only has meaning in terms of some ordered plan, some design, either felt or expressed, by which to measure transcendental deviance that is only a theological circumlocution for evil.

7

Death on Camera

MARTIN HEIDEGGER, the noted German philosopher has said that there is a marked difference between the existential fact of a person in the throes of death (e.g., I die—*ich sterbe*) and the abstract reference to death (e.g., one dies—*man stirbt*). Filmmakers such as Jean Cocteau (*Orpheus*) and Marcel Camus (*Black Orpheus*) have been aware of this distinction and have personified death in order to heighten the unspeakable anxiety it entails. Akira Kurosawa, for example, has said: "Sometimes I think of my death. I think of ceasing to be . . . and it is from these thoughts that *Ikiru* came."[1] Kurosawa's film on death has as its title *Ikiru*, the Japanese verb "to live." The plot centers about a "little man," little only in terms of epic stature but not within the context of the courage required to confront death squarely.

Kanji Watanabe (Takashi Shimura), works within a municipal bureaucracy. He learns that he will die within a year. Actually, as the narrator observes, he has been dead for twenty-five years within the tomb of petty officialdom. It is the sentence of death that is really a rebirth in terms of a new perspective on what a treasure life is. Watanabe's decision is to draw his money from the bank and take the velvet path of pleasure to the grave. The first half of the film treats his search for an existential life-before-death philosophy. He meets a writer who teaches him that it is a duty to enjoy life. The writer refers to himself in Faustian terms as a Mephistopheles, "but a good one who won't ask to be paid." A satanical symbol is present in the form of a black dog at his feet. Having been counselled that the greed to live is really a virtue, Watanabe, in the company of the writer, seeks to live the "sweet life." The night-life odyssey has elements of sadness similar to most of Fellini's night-club and party scenes. Subsequently, Watanabe befriends a girl in the office and their relationship is misunderstood by his son and wife. Through her he discovers a new zest for life, a desire to be of some use in life, perhaps even after death. She encourages him, although she cannot direct his efforts toward any precise avenue of altruism.

The second half of the film begins with Watanabe laid out on the funeral bier followed by a flashback to see what his irrevocable macrodecision was regarding his commitment to evil or the unifying good, love. He died in the snow, we learn from the office workers present at the wake. We also learn that he built a recreation park for children. We are shown Watanabe's determination to achieve the apparently simple task of building a park. We are in the presence again of the "big knife" mentioned earlier, the sharp double-edged antinomy of organizational inertia on the one hand and the transcendental voice of personal conscience on the other. Watanabe, in the face of death, heeds conscience and begins to vault over bureaucratic hurdles, and in so doing, he saves from oblivion a citizen's petition for a park. The grace of the film lies not in the event but as Edmund Burke has said: "The meanness of the business was raised by the dignity of the object."[2] The object in this case was dying well, as a man serving others.

Nevertheless, *Ikiru* still stays on this side of the grave. Only film fantasies such as *Stairway to Heaven* and *Here Comes Mr. Jordan* dare to traverse the Great Divide between life and death. Kurosawa once attempted a serious supernatural scene in *Rashomon*, but it was done within the frame of reference of a legend. The most that cinema can successfully do in this regard is, through empathy, to draw the audience to the very brink of the grave. One thinks of Barbara Stanwyck's acting tour de force in *Sorry, Wrong Number*, where the movieviewer is psychologically displaced into the claustrophobic situation of an invalid who hears a phone conversation concerning her murder. Trapped, she tries to call for help and convince persons that she is to be killed. Necessarily, the approach of death is telescoped into a much shorter compass of time than that in *Ikiru*. Though meant only to be an entertainment type of suspense thriller, *Sorry, Wrong Number* succeeds in making an important contribution to a cinematic theology of death by illustrating how approaching death can drain from a person's consciousness all life-related considerations. If war is the continuation of politics by other means, as von Clausewitz held, then death would seem to be but the continuation of human consciousness by other means, as freed from the gravitational forces of self-interest, the external distractions of one's milieu, and the fractured time-span of attention. In *Sorry, Wrong Number*, Barbara Stanwyck's victim has been hermetically sealed off from all time, space, and ego-related considerations but her own death. If death means anything phenomenologically, it is the relaxing of our psychic hold on all that is worldly and the sudden absorption into another life. The concentrated forms of attention on timeless realities in the spotlight of eternity, so essential to death in its role as a bridge from one form of consciousness to another, is found neither in *Ikiru* nor in *Sorry, Wrong Number*. The overwhelming number of films on death, even the artistically better ones, fall into the category of Heidegger's impersonal *man stirbt*. One thinks immediately of the "shoot-out," the "walk-down," the ambush, the littered battlefield, and the victims of science-fiction voyages. For all its footage on death, the motion picture industry has contributed comparatively little to an understanding of death as a theological horizon where two forms of consciousness blend, that of this world and that of the next.

The mingled emotional impact caused by impending death is made up of what we may call "loss" and "gain" elements. The loss of all to which man has grown attached in this life is the focus of a vast number of motion pictures on death, especially the suspenseful ones of an Alfred Hitchcock or a Henri Jacques Clouzot. Such directors are concerned with the secular "this-worldly" consequences of death and so address the theme from the negative side of the balance sheet. Despite being produced in a civilization at least theoretically based on an "other-worldly" revelation of man's immortality, most Western films support the clear inference that physical death is the first and only death. This is not the assumption of Scripture, which teaches that death is the first and, in itself, the least important of two deaths of which the second is the death of

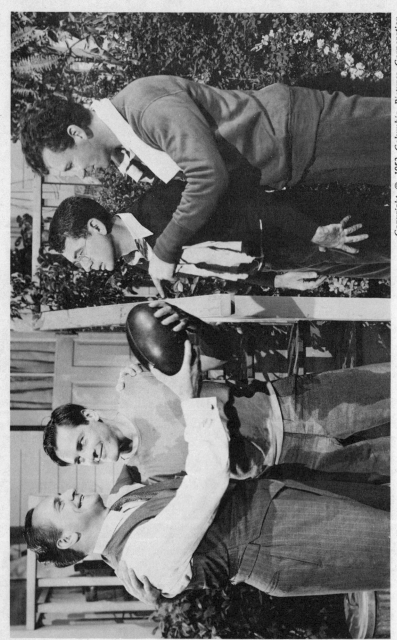

Frederic March and Arthur Kennedy in a scene from the Columbia Pictures Death of a Salesman.

the spirit. It is theologically revealing to consider the persons who die in films such as *The Brotherhood, The Magnificent Seven, The Wild Bunch* or the Italian-influenced Westerns such as *The Good, The Bad and the Ugly.* Do they die a truly human kind of death? Not if we compare their deaths to that of Gypo Nolan (Victor McLaglen) in *The Informer* of Yuri Zhivago in *Dr. Zhivago,* or of Joy Follett in *All the Way Home.* What is the difference? It is a profound philosophical one that the German language stresses by providing two distinct verbs describing death: that of an animal (*krappieren*) and that of a human being (*sterben*). Many screen deaths are glorified instances of animal deaths with no thought either to after-life or to a continuance of consciousness but in another modality. The striking quality of the stark Scandinavian film, Henning Carlsen's *Hunger,* lies precisely in concentrating on the animal level of existence and the slow dying that is a state of extreme malnutrition. As a total experience, death is a metabiological reality.

The early Russian filmmakers showed sensitivity to the spiritual dimension of human dying not only as a loss in terms of biological continuity but also regarding the quality of consciousness. In the case of Alexander Dovzhenko's *Earth,* a tractor is the hero of the film as the social talisman of prosperity, community solidarity and social order. The final scene shows the fragility of human life. Dovzhenko's protagonist, Vassily, the good-humored and upright young party chairman, is on his way home one night, doubly elated by having met the village's problems and the prospect of seeing his awaiting bride. All nature joins his effervescent mood: the moon, birds, cattle, and the beasts of the field. The chairman breaks out into a dance of exaltation along the road when suddenly he crumples, shot dead by the Kulak whose land his tractor has invaded.

The key to Dovzhenko's film philosophy is the ancient belief in death as the link in the renewal process of nature. Human life is fertile as is mother earth, but as in nature living things die to enable new forms of life, so too in human affairs.[3] The death of Vassily is not a futile one; it is, as one would naturally expect from a dialectic philosophy, a union of opposites. His mourners pay no attention to the confession of his murderer; they are united with the earth which at the time of the funeral receives Vassily's body.

In regard to this masterwork of Dovzhenko, Mircea Eliade makes some pertinent observations in his book, *The Sacred and Profane*. Talking of the belief of death as found in the rites of the earth mother as the central mystery of the world and linked with regenerative life, he says:

Life comes from somewhere that is not this world and finally departs from here and goes to the beyond, in some mysterious way continues in an unknown place unaccessible to the majority of mortals. Human life is not felt as a brief appearance in time, between one nothingness and another; it is preceded by a pre-existence and continued in post-existence. Little is known about these two extraterrestrial stages of human life, yet they are known to *exist*. Hence for religious man, death does not put a final end to life. Death is but another modality of human existence.[4]

Dovzhenko's film poetry brings this point out vividly since its underlying premise was that shared by most primitive cultures whose animism saw the cosmos divided into a visible reality and an unseen superreality. Neolithic burial customs and rites are akin to that presented in *Earth*, a rite of spirit-worship, of belief in the cult of the dead and the continuance of man's soul in some mysterious higher plan beyond evil, beyond human comprehension.[5]

In effect, we see how much in tune with the timeless rhythms of the universe are the concepts of death when seen as a cycle of hope in Dovzhenko's works: *Zvenigora, Aerograd, Shchors,* and *Michurin*. In these films, death as loss is merely a prelude to rebirth, a theme, as Eliade has indicated, common to the philosophy of Socrates, to Buddhism, to the Hindu sacrificer and to Alexandrian Judaism and Pauline Christian theology.[6]

This ancient worldview of death, still common to preindustrial peoples, is not implied in most contemporary films which incorporate the *man stirbt* theme of Heidegger. What is interesting to see is that the true change in spiritual consciousness, incumbent upon death, has been anticipated in most films of the sixties that show people living their second death parallel with their physical existence. Psychologists call this condition alienation; religious thinkers would call it a foretaste of hell. In any event theologians would do well to explore this phenomenon of the hemorrhaging of being from an existentialist viewpoint.[7] Here film can help to furnish a catalog of concrete instances.

Laslo Benedek's film of Arthur Miller's play *Death of a Salesman*, stars Fredric March as Willy Loman. Willy is a salesman who lives a roseate dream quite foreign to the sawtooth realities of life ("A salesman's gotta dream; it comes with the territory"). He is unconscious of the social and economic forces that shape his role in life as breadwinner, as father, as husband, as man. He is to American culture in the early postwar years what Sinclair Lewis's Babbitt was to that same culture in the pre-Depression era. Both are types, to be sure, but types with numerous living counterparts readily identifiable in our business society.

Willy Loman, even more than Kanji Watanabe in *Ikiru*, has been dead for twenty-five years not because his life, like that of the petty Japanese bureaucrat, is unexciting, monotonous, empty of any dramatic social relevancy. Loman is dead spiritually because he cannot be reached by other human beings. The delicate relationship of Watanabe to the young girl in the first half of Kurosawa's film is an awakening, a part of nature's regenerative cycle even in the area of the life spirit. Willy Loman nowhere gives evidence of this type of rebirth. His son, Biff, has to wound his father verbally in order to make him attentive to the mere words he is speaking. Biff is decidedly more "inner-directed" than Willy in a curious reversal of David Riesman's categories regarding more the "mass media–conditioned" generation of the forties.[8] Biff's lead remarks in their encounter are: "Let's hold on to the facts tonight. We're not going to get anywhere bullin' around." But Willy is beyond communication of any meaningful sort. Consequently Biff is compelled to puncture the balloon of his father's solipsistic world, crying out: "Pop, I'm a dime a dozen, and so are you!" Willy, shaken by the remark, retorts in an uncontrolled outburst: "I am not a dime a dozen; I am Willy Loman, and you are Biff Loman." The answer of Biff is firm: "I am not a leader of men, Willy, and neither are you. You were never anything but a hard-working drummer who landed in the ashcan like all the rest of them; I'm one dollar an hour, Willy. I tried seven states and couldn't raise it. A buck an hour!" Willy can only reply in anger: "You vengeful, spiteful mutt!" Biff, almost in tears, cries out: "Pop. I'm nothing. I'm nothing, Pop. Can't you understand that? There's no spite in it anymore. I'm just what I am, that's all." As Biff begins to sob, Willy asks his wife why. Then Biff utters the plaintive words, "Will you let me go, for Christ's sake? Will you take that phony dream and burn it before something happens?"

The theological implications here indicate a reduction to some lower level of human existence, a cellar type of consciousness that is more instinct-motivated than rationally directed. The continuity of nature is broken, it seems, since human existence is incapable of developing its latent communicative power substantially beyond that of animals. What else does transcendence mean if not an openness to values, to the spiritual powers of perception regarding the hidden but not indecipherable meaning in the cryptic Persian rug that is the ordered system of the universe? Death as a bridge between forms of human consciousness leads either to a higher or lower form of sustained consciousness. The death of animals (*krappieren*) is not of the same significance as that of humans (*sterben*) precisely because animals are dumb (they speak not because they hear not).[9] The spiritual capacity to hear means much more than the mere physical registering of sound waves set in motion.

Death seen in terms of alienation, in terms of the undeveloped or even repressed powers to hear in terms of spiritual receptivity, is a common theme in motion pictures. One might say that the secular language for expressing death has been reduced to the aborted life of spiritual consciousness, even conscience, as the narrow catwalk that leads over the chasm of physical death into the new form of consciousness, that rebirth that Eliade has associated with certain Greek, Hindu, Buddhist, Hebraic and Christian traditions. There are many films of the 1960s that have treated the death theme obliquely in terms of ruptured human communications: *Who's Afraid of Virginia Woolf?* (between husband and wife), *The Graduate* (between parents and children), *If . . .* (between school authorities and students), *Easy Rider* (between hippies and society), *Blow-Up* (between public opinion and personal experience), *The Loved One* (between the artist and his profession), *Burn!* (between the colonized and the conquerors), *Catch 22* (between soldier and his profession), and *Winterlight* (between the religious minister and his calling).

These films again describe the problem of the "big knife," conscience facing a mindless system. This time the antagonism takes a more expansive form: a cosmos of apparent absurdity. There is a kind of dying in each of the films just mentioned, a consciousness in transition to something firm, final, definitive. It is as if man committed to live his life forward knows he has lost the divine scent, to use the late C. S. Lewis's felicitous phrase.

This sense of a trail that man must ferret out through the dense thickets of life before it is too late is the concern of Ingmar Bergman's *Wild Strawberries*, in which the personal relevance of a human life and its contacts are tested by reference to death. Dr. Isak Borg, played by the former silent screen director, Victor Sjostrom, is a 78-year-old doctor who is journeying to Lund to be decorated by the university there. Accompanied by his daughter-in-law, Borg begins to go back in time. This is a Bergman characteristic: to displace physically a character in space as the occasion for a psychological displacement in time. We are treated to one of those rare cinematic studies of the state of a person's interior life. Three psychic currents converge in the old man's mind: the remarks of his daughter-in-law that he, like his son, is cold, impersonal, and basically selfish; the dream of the preceding night in which he sees himself in a coffin accidentally tipped over from a hearse; and the flashbacks of his early loves.

On occasion in each human life such circumstances converge to create vivid illumination of one's life in its entirety. Such is the case with Dr. Borg, for whom this illumination is a rehearsal for death as the great moment of truth. Three psychological mirrors serve to give Dr. Borg a rounded view of the meaning of his life. One mirror reflects what his motives have been; a second, what he has become; and a third, what repercussions these have had on others. These psychological mirrors take different forms: the subconscious awareness of death in a dream; the judgment passed by his daughter-in-law; and the review of his past in the light of both. Dr. Borg is on the trail; he has caught the "divine scent." Following it fearlessly he begins to realize how frail his achievements are. If death has any merit, it lies in its power to help man regain his direction on a spiritual trail often covered over by life's smaller concerns and more trivial commitments.

Parker Tyler comments on this point, musing on the spiritual attitude that stamps such a quiet impassive face as that of Dr. Borg. He calls it a "living mask" of a perishing consciousness, adding:

One wonders if this humanly complete mask can be achieved *without* "selfishness." It is true—a "family man" does have responsibilities to others; to his wife, his parents, his children. But he may not be strong enough to be himself and also give form and direction to even his closest of kin. It is the limitation of individual strength whose paths appears so movingly in Victor Sjostrom's face and figure.[10]

Death brings awareness of alternatives. That is why directors such as Jean-Luc Godard and Alain Resnais, following the pattern of Robbe-Grillet's novels, sometimes fuse the indicative mood of the present with the subjunctive mood of what might have been. Tyler misses the full dimension of choices open to a person such as Dr. Borg when he reduces all human choice to a single crucial decision: "to honor oneself with selfishness or to honor others with charity."[11] The problem is that Dr. Borg, like Watanabe in *Ikiru*, forgot how to live, how to love. Thinking back on how his brother stole from him the girl he wished to marry, Dr. Borg realizes that his flight into the medical profession was obsessive, draining time and energy from other more human interests and leaving him less warm, less simple, and less spontaneous than he could have been. Bergman focuses on a profound truth often missed in many American films of social protest, adventure, and escape, namely, that the overarching challenge is not that posed by the "big knife" dilemma that life in social systems raises. This can be unmasked, spoofed, and fled from in myriad ways. In the last analysis it is the "big knife" dilemma in which death, not conscience, brings authenticity to us whether we wish it or not. In other words, conscience cannot work except as a function of death. Even subconsciously, acts of conscience are rehearsals for the macrodecision implied in personal dying.

Bergman's *The Seventh Seal* is a stunning example of the one certitude, the inevitable crash of death's guillotine in the affairs of human beings. The allegorical story is set in medieval Sweden. A knight, Antonius Blok (Max von Sydow) returns from the crusades to encounter Death (Bengt Ekerot). Death refuses the knight the postponement he requests. As an alternative, the knight offers to play a game of chess; Death accepts. As the film unfolds the knight's moves to win are checked at every turn: a dead shepherd, victim of the bubonic plague; a traveling player with a death-bed mask; a painter finishing his canvas of the Danse Macabre; a monk in a confessional with the laugh of Death; outside the church an alleged sorceress condemned to be burned at the stake; an ex-seminarian now turned graverobber; the traveling players' show is interrupted by the chant of *Day of Wrath* and a procession of flagellants, one of them proclaiming the imminence of death.

Finally Death takes several chess pieces off the knight's chess-board. A traveling player climbs a tree to pass the night only to find

Courtesy: Fleetwood Films, Inc.

Vittorio de Sica's *Umberto D.*

Death sawing it down. The so-called sorceress is led to the stake when the knight asks her about God and the devil. Death berates him for always seeking answers. She is burned. The chess game is resumed. The ex-seminarian contracts the plague and goes off to die. When Death wins the chess game, Blok demands to know his secrets but he pretends to know nothing. A traveling player, a blacksmith and his wife, Blok, his courier, and a mute girl arrive at the knight's castle with the premonition of a cosmic catastrophe. The knight's wife reads from the Apocalypse while a storm rages outside. A knock is heard at the door three times but no one is there. Suddenly all look at the entrance and recognize Death (the audience sees only the alarmed faces of the occupants of the castle). The mute girl speaks at last: "All is consummated!" The next day the traveling player describes to his wife his vision of Death leading away the five persons who faced Death the previous day.

With Shakespearian splendor, *The Seventh Seal* presents medieval images with which Bergman was familiar in his childhood, as the son of a Lutheran pastor. The knight is he who seeks to know the ultimate questions. He is not afraid to die but really does not know for what one must live. Jacques Siclier, in his book on Ingmar Bergman, has argued eloquently that the key scene in the film is the knight's sharing of a meal in the country with the traveling player, his wife, and their small baby.[12] Whether they represent the Holy Family or not, one thing seems certain: they, of all the people, are immersed in life, not death. They are consecrated to life and through love to expanding the domain of life.[13] Except for them, Death stalks the scene reminding those of us living in a more skeptical, scientific age that we are not free of mass anxiety. Our fears, more pronounced among youth, issue not from a bubonic plague but from twentieth-century nuclear weapons. The medieval setting of *The Seventh Seal* should not blind us to the same apocalyptic mood of our own century.

Although *The Seventh Seal* preceded *Wild Strawberries*, it represents a theological advance over the latter, principally because Bergman tries to draw back the veil on the most universal and most decisive event in human life. In *Wild Strawberries* doubt is cast on all the accomplishments of life. It is the same genre of doubt posed in the other films mentioned above with the difference that in *Wild*

Strawberries a dream of death and advanced old age were the occasions for the doubts.

In *Umberto D* we see the same hourglass with its thrifty, ever-thinning reserve of sand. Vittorio de Sica's masterly protagonist is an elderly but distinguished gentleman, whose loneliness serves as a treatise on approaching death in mid-twentieth-century society. It is a harsh but frank film, one that was not popular at the box office. As with Antonioni in *La Notte*, de Sica studies the suffering and weakness of man in Chekhovian fashion, making us resonate with the feelings of the persons instead of judging them. Umberto D has no real friends, only his dog Flac. He lives in a twilight world, neither rejected by society nor integrated within it. He shares in the same uncertainty as the pregnant unwed mother, Maria. But the shadow of death, the ever-recurring break in human communications mentioned earlier, appears even here.

Exactly when Umberto loses his dog, Maria's lover steals away. Neither can rise above the personal distress that has overtaken them to enter into sympathy with the other. They, like Flac, are dumb. Not knowing how to hear, they cannot speak. Since the higher sphere of consciousness where the spirit is alert is closed, they live with the personal anxiety of the moment.[14] Their conscious state at that moment is less than human, less than kind. A neorealist such as de Sica is very likely suggesting that it is because a mechanical type of society has impeded them to respond any other way. Notwithstanding, de Sica's Umberto D is a fiercely independent person, both plucky and dignified. Herein lies the reason why this film represents a theological step beyond Kurosawa's *Ikiru*, Bergman's *Wild Strawberries* and *The Seventh Seal*. Umberto D is confronting the full implications of indifference to real spiritual life; he is willing to die the slow death, knowing that there is another life beyond the grave. Pauline Kael has shown how a seemingly helpless, pitiable man can transcend the barrenness of metropolitan *anomie:*

His alienation has such pride and spirit that he is not unworthy to stand as a symbol of man's fate. But men do not necessarily want to view their fate: this great, pure and compassionate work has been seen by only a few thousand people. Yet for those few—and their numbers grow each year—it may be a rare, transforming experience.[15]

Umberto D, for all his understandable weakness, is neither petty nor self-pitying. His fate, though less kind than that of Watanabe or of Dr. Borg, finds him fully prepared. He will rise above the circumstances.

If one asks where did the steel in Umberto's character come from, one must go back to the years of formation. While it is impossible to know with certainty what events helped train Umberto to withstand loneliness and adversity, one can readily understand how children, even at a tender age, become inured to the buffets of life. Children are exposed to the "big knife" dilemma earlier and earlier. Few realize how our societies construct rules with a decided bias in favor of adults. Gabriela Mistral, the Chilean Nobel Prize–winning poet, once observed how early certain types of lower class children lose the sparkle in their eye and the smile on their face. Such children are growing old prematurely; they become miniature Umberto D's or, as Pauline Kael has so aptly put it, theirs is "a picture of loneliness, but at the other end of the life-span."[16] Consider de Sica's earlier works, *The Children Are Watching Us*, and *Shoeshine*, in which sensitive, promising children are placed under a low ceiling of potential by self-indulgent adults motivated by pleasure-pain incentives and nothing more. Or look at the cruel film of Buñuel—*Los Olvidados (The Young and the Damned)*—in which Pedro lives in a Darwinian world of the Mexican slums where only the fittest survive. Or consider René Clement's classic, *Forbidden Games*, in which two French refugee orphans are separated after having lived, played, and suffered together. The final scene of the little girl shouting the name of the boy she may never see again is a heartrending scene, another reminder of the crisis in human communications, especially between children and adults. In all these films, the child protagonists are preparing for life as well as death. In effect, they must choose between two exclusive options, that of an animal type of survival consciousness or a type of transcendence. The former anticipates the animal death (*krappieren*), while the latter tends to a human death (*sterben*). One could make out a strong case that the children in the aforementioned films all choose the road of autodetermination as did the protagonists in *A Taste of Honey, The Loneliness of the Long Distance Runner*, and *Rebel Without a Cause*. In any event, some rewarding theological discussion could be centered on such children's films as these.

The martyr's death has been discussed elsewhere in considering *The Passion of Joan of Arc* and *A Man for All Seasons*. One could add the fictional but saintly death of Billy Budd (Terence Stamp) in Peter Ustinov's film based on Herman Melville's novel of that name. Another similar transparent death is that of the shepherd Manolios (Pierre Vaneck) in Jules Dassin's *He Who Must Die*, based on Nikos Kazantzakis's novel. This film will be discussed at greater length in the chapter on sacrificial love. Suffice it to say that Manolios's death is one that, in its free acceptance for motives of faith and charity, leaves unambiguous the new mode of consciousness for which death is ordinarily only an incident, a doorway. In the martyr's case the death itself is a preview of the new modality of consciousness.

Each man, as we well know, dies his own death. Is death only what Hamlet referred to as a "sleep of dreams," that blessed alternative to existence? But Hamlet knows that conscience, the arbiter of the transcendental, makes cowards of us all. And so we go on suffering the slings and arrows of outrageous misfortune, pondering with Watanabe, Dr. Borg, the knight, and Umberto the great imponderable.

Once again the findings of this chapter can be expressed in six basic principles. First of all, there are two forms of death: one of sentient beings, animals, with a single mode of consciousness coterminous with life and ending in death; and another, that of beings whose decisions take place against a transcendental backdrop of good and evil. This implies that death, as the macrodecision, judges the quality of that life. *Ikiru, Wild Strawberries, The Seventh Seal,* and *Umberto D* all displayed characters with strong resolves in facing their rapidly approaching deaths. This human consideration of transcendence in, through and after death is highly personal, affirming another distinction, that of Heidegger's on the uniqueness and irreversibility of death (*ich sterbe* instead of *man stirbt*).

Secondly, although each man dies his own death unassisted and unaccompanied in his moment of truth, there are experiences of empathy that simulate the liberation from all earthbound distractions (e.g., *Sorry, Wrong Number*). That is to say, an existential theology of death can find great support in the many films that stress the "loss" element of death in the binomial "loss-gain." The "loss" impact must not only consist of the temporal cessation of consciousness with its historical contents (*The Magnificent Seven*, *The Wild Bunch*, *The Good, the Bad and the Ugly*, *The Brotherhood*). That alone would be an animal demise (i.e., *krappieren*). Also necessary for a rounded theology of death is the death of reconciliation as seen in *The Informer*, *All the Way Home*, and *Dr. Zhivago*. This is more of a human death in its higher transcendental sense (*sterben*).

Thirdly, dying in many of the world's religions has a common reference to rebirth, the second life, and immortality by a participation in the processes of nature. The Russian director, Alexander Dovzhenko, treated death as a theme in the ancient ritual sense of a "nature resurrection" (*Earth*).

Fourthly, films reflecting the urban industrial milieu of the mid-twentieth century show a discontinuity with the aforementioned concept of death as found in societies based on the virgin, prescientific state of nature. In contemporary Western civilization, the pain of loss, ordinarily associated with death, seems to be stretched out along the entire axis of human life in anxiety, alienation, ennui and solitude (*Death of a Salesman*, *The Entertainer*, *Winterlight*, *The Loved One*, and *Catch 22*). The irrationality and "sleepwalker" condition of the central characters in a growing number of films augurs a serious break in social and human communications as if the recent "death-of-God" movement meant disconnecting not only vertical lines of dialogue but horizontal ones as well (*Blow-Up*, *Who's Afraid of Virginia Woolf?*, *The Knack*, *Alfie*, *Morgan!*, *Darling*, *Charlie Bubbles*, *Billy Liar*). A distinct change—is it unfair to say "decline"?—in human consciousness has been registered. Theologically we must talk, therefore, of an obscured transcendental horizon, a pseudodeath that is more hazardous than the clarity that impending death mediated to Watanabe (*Ikiru*), Dr. Borg (*Wild Strawberries*), the knight (*The Seventh Seal*), and Umberto D himself.

Fifthly, death, as feared as it commonly is, can have the salutary effect of enabling man to reconstruct his life's direction, thus recovering the "divine scent." The eschatological films of Kurosawa,

Rod Steiger in *The Pawnbroker*.

Bergman, and de Sica are virtually inexhaustible resources for deepening an existential theology of death.

Sixthly, the "big knife" antinomy posed for youth by the adult establishment too often acts as a form of death on them (e.g., *Los Olvidados*). Some perish physically, others spiritually, leaving a charmed circle of purified youngsters who are prepared for a life of authenticity in an inauthentic world of random, often outmoded, customs and expectations. This type of psychic martyrdom is implicit in the new forms of spiritual awareness of the young protagonists in films such as *The Children Are Watching Us, Shoeshine*, and *Forbidden Games*. This martyrdom is only, of course, a foreshadowing of the real martyrdom in which transcendence appropriates death as its form of witness rather than life (*Billy Budd, He Who Must Die, The Passion of Joan of Arc*, and *A Man for All Seasons*).

8

Grace on the Screen

ONE OF THE finest cinematic experiences of transcendence is to be found in the unforgettable role of Rod Steiger in Sidney Lumet's *The Pawnbroker*. The performance is so rich, so nuanced, that we may miss the interplay of two psychic phenomena. The first is the traumatic experiences of horror in the Nazi concentration camps that makes the protagonist, to quote Pauline Kael "unable to feel again, deadened, past pain, past caring."[1] The other noteworthy phenomenon is the determined will to remain human despite the subhuman conditions of Spanish Harlem where his pawnshop is located. In an earlier chapter on the pressure which society exerts on human transcendental impulses, I mentioned that human life can be extinguished as effectively through an ill-designed environment as through direct physical violence, even though the process may be slower. *The Pawnbroker* is the textbook case study of this principle. The cogent lesson of the film lies in the double capability of Steiger's pawnbroker to survive not only the violence of the Nazi police state but also the unintended consequences, almost as brutal, of urban blight.

Sol Nazerman is a Jew, a man who once loved and had that love snuffed out cruelly precisely because he was a Jew. When we meet the pawnbroker early in the film we recognize his hypersensitivity. He is a mimosa plant that quivers at every alien touch no matter how light. Whether he was always a sensitive person, more vulnerable to harsh words than the ordinary person, we shall never really know. All we know is that since the loss of his wife and other beloved kin and friends, the intermittent flashes of memory he has serve as an instant horror replay, invading him with pain and disgust. This memory track of past brutality gradually becomes synchronized with another visual track, that of the ongoing institutional violence all around him. The loneliness which Steiger represents is of a peculiar sort. It is due to the fact that he has spiritual sight, one could say a theological imagination. Pierre Teilhard de Chardin once remarked about his parallel vision of evolution and theology: "My God, am I the only one who sees?" So too, our pawnbroker is a seer, a solitary seer with a vision of what was, what is, and what ought to be.

Human beings have a way of deviating from certain predictable patterns of behavior. Unlike the sciences dealing with natural phenomena—chemistry, physics, biology, and so on—the study of human nature is distinctive in that the statistical regularities that it follows in the aggregate yield no certainty of how this concrete person in this set of existential circumstances will perform. He may perform far below or far above the modal norm of expectancy. We saw in the chapter on evil how this dynamic "downward resourcelessness" is possible in the area of both individual and institutional behavior. Here I wish to treat another form of religious deviance, performance beyond the expectations of typical role behavior as socially transmitted over the generations. In general, religious cultures agree on such things as reverence for parents, for country, for the unfortunate, compliance with duty, and the concern for one's rights to life, liberty, and property as well as the rights of others. The point of prime relevance to us here is a transcendence beyond one's role, one's duty, one's pattern of socially derived expectations so that a quantum leap in the quality of human performance is achieved, a leap that is visible and historically palpable. *The Pawnbroker* certainly exemplifies such a leap.

That some divine motivation is at work in the life of the traumatized pawnbroker seems a valid inference. Sol Nazerman's pattern of behavior is extraordinarily atypical. He does not run away, though physically he could. He remains with the suffering residents of the ghetto and all that they signify: hunger, broken dreams, and the shameless "flesh-peddling." No, he does not flee. In fact, there is no evidence in the film that he even entertains the thought. He stays and accepts his place in a dark environmental dungeon. A daytime inhabitant in a blighted neighborhood, the pawnbroker manages to resist those compromises that subhuman living standards make appear attractive. Why, one asks. Mere psychological and sociological explanations are not sufficient. There must be some other source of strength, some divine uplift. This is not out of place for a man who has not broken faith either with his religious tradition, with his memory of loved ones, or with himself.

A careful viewing of *The Pawnbroker* shows us a man with remarkable continuity of character and consistency of behavior, two traits that are salient in clearly religious contexts such as that of the martyred Lutheran minister of World War II in *Pastor Hall* and the unshaken prince of the Church, imprisoned by the Communists in *The Prisoner*. There seems little hesitancy to admit that, in the case of these two martyr types, they lived under what the Quakers call a "divine covering." Likewise, one can logically infer that the central character in *The Pawnbroker* has always been a receipient of divine favors. There is a reason for this.

The pawnbroker's life is full of convergent bits of evidence that reveal a tendency away from self-seeking. Nowhere do we notice either resentment or hate; repulsion and anger exist, to be sure, but no vindictiveness is shown. If we inventory the qualities of character that Rod Steiger incarnates in this memorable role, the list is impressive: the stolid acceptance of his unmerited image as a penny-pinching shrewd Jewish businessman; his mercy and kindness, begrudging as it may seem through his impassive face and gestures; his resistance to sexual libertinage, in part for traumatic reasons, in part due to principles; his sympathy for poorly educated, intellectually inferior lower class Puerto Ricans and Negroes; his courage in the face of danger (i.e., resisting the "hold-up" thugs); and a heroic perseverance, despite everything, in faith in both man and God.

Cinematically speaking *The Pawnbroker* may fall short of being great, but Rod Steiger's characterization does not. He has given not only a demonstration of acting virtuosity but also a rich phenomenological study of the compenetration of psychology and grace. *The Pawnbroker* is as central a contribution to a behavioral theology as could be hoped for. Moreover, its relevance is enhanced by its addressing itself to a key issue of our emerging world civilization: the inhumanity of manmade environments to their inhabitants, necessarily frustrated in any efforts to surpass themselves and evolve humanly.

The avenues of grace are many. *The Pawnbroker* treated a more delicate, less spectacular, form of grace. There are other manifestations of God's unbidden workings in human lives that produce a certain inspiring synergism so that the sum total of a person's action is not explained by such components as rational calculation, psychological motivation, social expectations, or mere physiological stimuli of pain and pleasure. The cinema has left us uplifted on several occasions by grace-laden acts of mercy, pardon, trust, or self-sacrifice: Mrs. McPhillips's forgiveness of Gypo Nolan's betrayal of her son, Frankie, in *The Informer;* the Bishop's reluctance to disclose Jean Valjean's theft of one of his gold candlesticks in *Les Misérables;* the incriminating silence of a priest out of respect for the seal of confession in *I Confess;* the willingness of a killer (James Cagney) to thwart teenage hero-worship by simulating cow-

Courtesy: Allied Artists.

Terence Stamp in *Billy Budd*. An Allied Artists Release.

ardice on his way to the electric chair in *Angels with Dirty Faces;* the heroic filibuster of the junior Senator (James Stewart) in Frank Capra's *Mr. Smith Goes to Washington;* the blessing of the saintly sailor on his judge, Captain De Vere, in *Billy Budd;* the humility and compassion of the industrialist for the underprivileged kidnaper in *High and Low;* the newspaperman's acceptance of the marrige of his daughter to a Negro in *Guess Who's Coming to Dinner,* and the prosecutor's courage in booking the conspiring Greek generals in Costa Gavras's *Z.* These are some instances of human response to the legally unenforceable.

The question of grace is intimately connected with that of charity, the most fragrant in the bouquet of virtues. In the film of Christian Jaque, *If All the Guys in the World . . . ,* a fishing vessel off the coast of Norway is threatened with an epidemic. Furthermore, there is some interracial tension between a North African steward and the second mate. There is only a single reasonable alternative open since the ship cannot reach any port within two days—a ham radio appeal for help. Luckily, it is picked up in Togo, Africa, by Italian colonists who arrange to have medicine sent out. Meanwhile, a remote diagnosis by wireless radio is initiated despite a raging storm that threatens to interrupt the contact. The medical reports determine that the sailors fell sick from food poisoning due to a bad meal they had eaten. There is only twelve hours for the crew to be saved by an injection of serum which only the Pasteur Institute in Paris has.

The race against the clock begins. In Paris, Jean Louis, a young radio ham obtains the serum and has it sent to Germany by airplane. He then radios another amateur in Munich who establishes contact with the Berlin airport, thanks to his daughter's boy friend, an American soldier. Since the airplane lands in East Berlin, the Russians obtain the serum and pick up the baton in the crucial relay race. Under government orders, a Russian airplane carries the serum to Copenhagen where it is taken by Air France to Oslo. The medicine is finally brought to the ship by a special Norwegian plane. Suddenly, the wind carries the precious packet into the sea. The North African sailor comes to the rescue. Being a Mohammedan, he is the only healthy member of the crew since he did not eat the spoiled ham. He heroically dives into the ocean and retrieves the life-saving serum. The film ends with a moving reception by the inhabitants of the port of destination.

Although *If All the Guys in the World . . .* is a melodrama with not a few contrived moments of suspense, it does present a very credible account of how contagious charity can be. The spirit of fraternity and service that exists among radio hams is one of the finest transnational realities in a troubled world of exaggerated nationalisms and cultural biases. What is remarkable, however, is how the indifference and egoism of those touched by this spirit quickly vanish. Most people are accustomed to live within equivocal social systems where good and evil coexist and where self-interest is accepted as a common norm of behavior. The radio ham phenomenon is an unusual social invention of part-time *aficionados* who help to channel their altruistic energies, often repressed in their daily occupations, toward the service of others. Rarely are the transcendental impulses of good given such free play as in ham radio circles. We are in the presence of a vibrant collective motion of grace that has a peculiar ability to overcome the most calloused skeptics.

One more form of charity should be mentioned: the political visionary who dedicates himself to the task of uniting peoples for the purposes of greater order, stability and international solidarity. The film, *Wilson*, with Alexander Knox in the title role, is an example of political zeal beyond the call of duty or even high-minded statesmanship. It is Wilson who champions the cause of the League of Nations at the meeting of the Big Four in Paris, and who subsequently carries the cause to the American people when the Senate opposes the plan, refusing to ratify America's entry into the very body that Woodrow Wilson as President was instrumental in shaping. Evidence indicates a neurotic streak in Wilson.[2] Like Sol Nazerman, Wilson served transcendental designs despite psychic debilities.

When children read history books or are later disillusioned by cynical "Realpolitik" considerations in diplomacy and state affairs, they tend to forget that the area of politics is not impervious to the stirrings of idealism. If grace is idealism backed by hard conviction in the face of obstacles and ridicule, Wilson (Alexander Knox) demonstrates its practical exercise in his barnstorming trip around the United States, trying to convince the people of the need for United States participation in the League of Nations. As history shows, he failed and in so doing brought on the stroke that certainly shortened his life. Political labels, partisan considerations, and the intrigues of international diplomacy should not close off an existential theology of grace from studying this realm as a focus of supernatural inspiration. The inspiration to carry on must come from sources deeper than those ordinarily at work in the sphere of politics (e.g., prestige, profit and power). Seen in this light, *Wilson* demonstrates grace at work in the common clay of a statesman who succeeded in channeling his energies, even those neurotic, into constructive pathways.

Because inspiring biographical films like *Wilson* are rare in terms of a theology of politics, mention should be made of *Lawrence of Arabia*.[3] The enigmatic figure of the archaeologist turned revolutionary is splendidly acted by Peter O'Toole. Set against the backdrop of a nomadic Bedouin tribal existence, Lawrence sparks the Arab revolt against the Turks, who in World War I, were allied with the Central Powers. The same disillusion of the scholar and idealist that *Wilson* brought out recurs here as Lawrence's vision is shattered on the rocks of power politics and personal degradation in a Turkish dungeon. The flogging and insinuated homosexual treatment by the Turkish Bey, the Sykes-Picot Agreement of England that took the just fruits of the Arabs away from them and the apathy and petty factionalism of the Arabs—all conspired to turn Lawrence away from the public scene. As Shaw he enlisted in the Air Force and died while veering his motorcycle away from two boys in his path. Like the central figure in *The Pawnbroker*, Lawrence was clearly a psychologically wounded person; many theories, some conflicting, exist on this point. Nevertheless, resorting again to argument by inference, the presence, not of a "downward resourcelessness," but rather of a divine covering seems to emerge from the convergence of probabilities in Lawrence's life, faithfully recreated by Robert Bolt's script and David Lean's direction. In a similar vein as *Wilson* and *Lawrence of Arabia* is *The Shoes of the Fisherman*, in which Anthony Quinn plays a type of Pope John XXIII, who in the face of a Red Chinese threat to launch atomic warfare pledges the riches of the Church to alleviate the oppressive economic conditions there. Here is a case, fictitious though it may be, of charisma in church statesmanship.

Consider now grace as it works in conversion. The spiritual life is classically thought of as a binary system, either a positive or negative valence with no intervening middle ground. In the Christian religion this is carried to the logical consequence of a judgment in the hereafter wherein the soul is confirmed either in good, thus meriting eternal happiness (either before or after purgatory), or evil, thus deserving eternal chastisement. Game theorists would call this a "zero-sum game," where all is lost or all is gained.

With this prelude, we can now discuss Federico Fellini's *La Dolce Vita*. Without some awareness of the Christian assumptions just mentioned one would forfeit a deeper understanding of the subliminal plot of grace working in the soul of an Italian journalist. As played by Marcello Mastroianni, Marcello, in covering the Via Veneto, takes the viewer with him on an odyssey through seven nights and seven dawns in the Eternal City. These scenes, generally conceded to be based on Fellini's early days as a journalist, appear between a prologue and an epilogue. The prologue shows a gilded statue of Christ borne by a helicopter over the dome of St. Peter's and over the rooftops of modern houses where girls sunbathe in skimpy bikinis. One shouts: "Oh, look, here comes Jesus!" Another replies: "Where's He going?" The epilogue is equally disturbing. After a night-long orgy attended by transvestites, pederasts, and nymphomaniacs, the guests wander down to the ocean's edge where excited fishermen are pulling in a sea monster whose large Cyclopean eye fills the screen. Both prologue and epilogue are filled with the dread of judgment, with "zero-sum" implications. The film has seven chapters, in effect, enclosed within the apocalyptic bookends of the helicopter-borne Christ and the giant eye.

The details of the scenario of *La Dolce Vita* are not of primary concern here. What is, however, of interest are the inner thoughts of Marcello. At each dawn he sees the events of the previous night in a different perspective. Dawn is light and light is the expression for coming to God. There is an unmistakable pattern in *La Dolce Vita*, an inner rhythm of beckoning hope and resigned acquiescence in weakness spelled out in seven distinct episodes. On the checkerboard of days and nights, Marcello vacillates between his "downward resourcelessness" and a transcendental commitment in terms of the rebirth discussed in the chapter on death. Marcello is on the divine scent but is too weak yet to follow the uphill, rocky path it leads to.

The final scene of the Umbrian maid waving to the blasé Marcello is a puzzle to most reviewers who pass over it.[4] Fellini is reported to have said that his ideal of God's attitude toward man is represented in the pleasant, smiling face of the innocent young girl and her attempts to communicate above the roar of the surf.[5] The futile abortive gesture of Marcello toward her as a beautiful girl leads him away is his way of postponing a decision. And the girl —she continues to smile, unperturbed. In *La Dolce Vita,* grace waits: it is patient; it is polite. The poignancy of the film is that the spiritual melody lingers on even though the music of the plot ceases. Who knows, perhaps some dawn on the Via Veneto Marcello may allow the "knife of conscience" to sink in or perhaps in the Umbrian refuge amid quiet and the hills he may see the young waitress again and feel a remorse, cooperating with the grace she certainly symbolizes in this theological masterwork of the screen.

If *La Dolce Vita* shows "grace toward conversion" within a Christian frame of reference, Kurosawa's *Red Beard* illustrates the "grace of conversion" in a contemporary Eastern—perhaps neo-Buddhist—context. Buddhism is the search for Enlightenment, an inner rebirth. In this sense *Red Beard* is a story of wisdom, not just the learning of abstract intellectual truths that lead to what D. H. Lawrence has called "mindlessness," an absence from what one is doing. *Red Beard* fits perfectly the description given by D. T. Suzuki, the noted Zen Buddhist teacher, who has written: "The supreme mark of the thoroughly integrated man is to be without a divided mind."[6] Red Beard (Toshiro Mifune), the name for the dedicated doctor-hero, is such a thoroughly integrated man.[7] He becomes the teacher and superior of a young intern who, aspiring to be part of the court medical staff, finds himself assigned to a state clinic. Shocked, the young man, Yuzo Kayama, deliberately breaks hospital rules, will not wear a uniform, and trespasses on forbidden areas reserved for insane patients. He undergoes a humiliating experience with one such patient that nearly costs him his life. This is his psychological breakthrough; he begins to take an interest in the hospital with its understaffed personnel, its overcrowded conditions and misery everywhere. Kayama soon learns that medical theory deals with Heidegger's *man stirbt* and not with the personal anguish of the dying patients he must attend. His education—in spiritual terms, his conversion—is beginning in earnest. As Donald Richie observes:

Kayama learns that . . . what he had always thought himself (upright, honest, hard-working) must now be reconciled with what he finds himself to also be (arrogant, selfish, insincere), and, the most important, that evil itself is the most humanly common thing in the world; that *good* is uncommon.[8]

The agent of change in the process is clearly Red Beard, the saintly doctor who lives the truth. He is unquestionably what Christians term a saint, despite the violent scene where in righteous anger he breaks the limbs of the sinister bouncers in the brothel. Some critics may think Red Beard sentimental, full of bathos, Dickensian in his vindication of good. However, that indicates how influenced we are by contemporary industrial civilization with its morally ambiguous and psychologically cautious "half-heroes."

The real truth of *Red Beard*—a recurring theme in Oriental religious practice as well as in most Kurosawa films—is that we must unlearn before we really learn, that we must be committed to some concrete task of service such as Watanabe's park project in *Ikiru* or the radio hams in *If All the Guys in the World . . .* before we comprehend what is good. Maybe that is what was lacking in Marcello in *La Dolce Vita*, some firm but kindly master who could have handed him a broom and said: "Sweep out that poor cripple's hovel." The knowledge of transcendental power always comes with its exercise, not before. Kayama no longer wants to join the Shogun's court medical staff but, contrary to even Red Beard's own wishes, wants to continue working at the clinic. The picture ends where it began with Kayama disobeying Red Beard, but now for different motives. He has found an ideal and nothing can shake him, not even Red Beard himself. As Donald Richie points out, the contagious attitude of Red Beard, his hatred of disease and its consequences, spread to Kayama so that "he *becomes* Red Beard, a thing which the other intern notices when toward the end of the

Courtesy: Robert Bresson.

Claude Laydau in *Diary of a Country Priest.*

film, he says: 'You know, you already talk just like Red Beard.' "[9]

The most exquisite expression of grace is that which works to confirm a person already on the high road of holiness. Undoubtedly the finest film on the temptations, met within a profound interior life of cooperation with grace, is Robert Bresson's film about Georges Bernanos's *Diary of a Country Priest.* The film is a profound cinematic study of grace not as merely beckoning the stray sheep (*La Dolce Vita*) or as converting the skeptical and disbelieving (*Red Beard*), but precisely as confirming one already holy in grace. Since, moreover, this film has many valuable references of a social and psychological nature; it is an excellent compendium of many of the principles discussed earlier.

Claude Laydu, in a remarkable performance, plays the Curé d'Ambricourt, whose first assignment in a rural parish depresses him because of the general atmosphere of spiritual torpor that he finds there. The Curé is one of those rare ascetical types whom nonbelievers find fascinating and whom comfortable Christians find disturbing. He is a "total giver," a person whose rule of life is "in for a penny, in for a pound." His "other-worldliness" is countered by the mediocrity and sullenness of all about him. The opening scene with the Count and his mistress embracing behind the grille conveys an intense physicality, an atmosphere of opaque materialism that stands in contrast to the transparency of the priest's intentions.[10] The Count is seen as stolid and impervious to light like the Romanesque monasteries of the tenth century; the Curé is Gothic in appearance: slender, translucent, and pointing beyond to eternity.

The plot is more complex than that of *Red Beard.* Basically, the story is of a French village curé, his older priestly colleague, and the members of a family of nobility who live in the local castle. The Count's mistress is the governess of his daughter, who herself knows of the triangle and thus is disgusted with life. The Countess is indifferent to life, having become embittered by the previous death of a baby. The priest is caught in unpleasant circumstances: the daughter's intention to commit suicide, the Countess's wavering faith and the sinful state of the Count and the governess. Having reconciled the Countess to God before her sudden death, the priest finds himself accused of causing it. The Curé refuses to defend himself, choosing not to produce a last letter from the Countess that would exonerate him before the Count, his daughter, and his superior. Bresson allows us to sense in the impassive face of this priest, lost in a maze of worldiness, the mystical depths of those who must pass through the dark night of the soul, where, as F. Scott Fitzgerald once said, "it is always one o'clock in the morning." The priest is besieged by despair; in addition to his frail health, he must contend with threats of suicide by the Count's daughter, sharp remarks from the villagers, and the shock of discovering that an old friend from his seminary days is living with a mistress (who, incidentally, cares for the Curé when he falls ill). Finally, in the throes of death the Curé exhorts his priest-friend to call on the pastor. His last words are: "All is grace!" Although less dramatic and less historical, Bresson's *Diary of a Country Priest* ranks with *The Passion of Joan of Arc* and *A Man for All Seasons* as rich sources for an existential theology, demonstrating that there are motions of grace that can carry persons beyond the ultimate test of endurance. That such cooperation with grace is uncommon may be more a problem of man's disposition than of God's limited budgeting of a boundless spiritual resource. This was poignantly seen in *King*, a documentary on Martin Luther King, Jr.

Admittedly the most intangible and yet most real force in any religious life, grace seems to hide itself in deeds. If we note its absence on the screen it may be because contemporary man does not prime his spiritual potential with deeds but contents himself to wait to see what the social fashion dictates. It should be clear that grace rarely calls the human spirit to what is fashionable. If we wish to put down a basic principle for a cinematic theology of grace, it is that the good flourishes on what to the worldly minded people is arid, unpromising soil. Throughout this chapter we have seen human endurance taxed through physical, psychological, and social pressures: the pawnbroker by the human destruction of the past and the environmental violence of the present; the psychological pressures of those who resent so-called "do-gooders" (*If All the Guys in the World . . .*, *Wilson*, and *The Shoes of the Fisherman*); the political opportunism and hypocrisy against persons of conscience and dedication (*The Passion of Joan of Arc*, *A Man for All Seasons*, and *Lawrence of Arabia*); the fear of breaking with habit, with one's circle of friends, with the familiar and the successful (*La Dolce Vita* and *Red Beard*); and, finally, the divine crucible of purification where the sanctified person is grieved because he sees under the light of eternity what others miss, namely the game of games, the spiritual life with its higher set of rules apprehended by relatively few and even only dimly (*Diary of a Country Priest.*).

The second principle would be that we can argue to the workings of grace by means of inference or by what John Henry Cardinal Newman called the "illiative sense." The test, as Newman knew, is subjective. Still the test, as subjective as it is, has objective boundaries. In the films just cited all are good men and women, even Marcello. Of course, he could be better and hopefully will be if he escapes the sexualized aura of the Via Veneto. But in all these case studies there were magnetic lines of force indicating that grace was working.

The third contribution to a theology of grace is that the modality of grace is necessarily freedom. This phenomenon is seen in Fellini's explanation of the final scene, with the innocent maid of Umbria trying to communicate to Marcello. At that moment it was an abortive dialogue with a deaf man; it is plain that the obstacle is not the waves' roar but Marcello's inner turmoil. Nevertheless the girl smiles and takes no umbrage at Marcello's reluctance to overcome the relatively short distance that would make personal conversation possible. This freedom, as Fellini deftly insinuates, is essential to the notion of grace as something offered—unbidden, unmerited, unexpected, and often unconscious in its operations. If the workings of grace are less clear in films such as *The Pawnbroker* and *Lawrence of Arabia*, it is because of the psychic background of the protagonists. Even in the case of *Diary of a Country Priest* there are certain psychological antecedents at work in the Curé d'Ambricourt that reflect the moods and attitudes of both the original author, Georges Bernanos, and the film's director, Robert Bresson, persons who tilt more toward the theological rigors of an extreme Roman Catholic orthodoxy than the latitude found in most Protestant writers. In any event, whatever the shades of confessional differences in defining freedom and grace's impact on it, there must be a submitting will if any divine fruit is to be borne.

A fourth observation would have to be the social communication

of grace, mainly by the example of those who have freely coope-
rated with grace. This question of the "multiplier effect" that is
obvious in the area of evil deserves more theological reflection
regarding the inner dynamic of the good to diffuse itself. At times,
the effects of grace work with a "time delay" as in the cases of St.
Joan of Arc and St. Thomas More, both of whose condemnatory
sentences were subsequently reversed by world public opinion.
Often, however, the example of others—in matters not having to
do with martyrdom, obviously—bears more immediate fruit. One
thinks of the radio hams (*If All the Guys in the World . . .*), of the
largesse of a Pope in the face of mass misery (*The Shoes of the
Fisherman*), of the inspired intern (*Red Beard*), and of the saintly
doctor in *The Albert Schweitzer Story.*

Fifthly, while grace can cascade once it reaches a certain critical
mass, the initial struggle to overcome the inertia of others, even
their hostility and duplicity, means that grace needs a new psychic
environment favorable to its growth. The persons who are loners
in the search for an authentic commitment to others and to God
must draw from other sources deeper than themselves. In the film
lives of St. Joan, St. Thomas More, Wilson, Lawrence, Sol Nazerman (the pawnbroker), and Anthony Quinn's charismatic Pope,
there is insinuated some process of constant regeneration of motives either through prayer, memories, renewed self-conviction or
direct revelation (e.g., the voices of St. Joan of Arc). Indispensable
in adverse conditions, the spread of the effects of grace in social
customs and enduring cultural forms—i.e., the "faith of our fathers"—poses a threat to the original inspiration in terms of milieu
religion. This was the obstacle to the Curé d'Ambricourt—the
weight of an institutional structure such as the Christian rural parish that rested on the earlier, fecund "multiplier effect" of other
inspired Christians.

Sixthly, the same case of the Curé d'Ambricourt argues for a
transcendental potential in man. True, it is seldom actuated as in
the case of the Curé d'Ars, of Mahatma Gandhi, of Albert
Schweitzer, and of an Einstein in his pacifism. Nevertheless, there
is hope for contemporary man, so powerful in the aggregate, so
impotent in the singular. The behavioral sciences often give an
unflattering image of man and so lead to the conclusion that he is

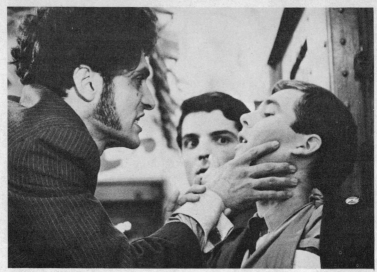

Larry Peerce's *The Incident.* An Allied Artists Release.

Michele Morgan in a scene from the Columbia Picture *The Proud and the Beautiful.*

a victim of his pretensions and nowhere more than in the field of religion. What behavioral scientists cannot research to their satisfaction is the submissive will, which disposes grace to work and bear its fruit. Certainly it is an effete humanism that would deny God the right, at critical junctures in history, to call on certain select human beings to discover the divine scent not only for themselves personally but to serve as pathbreakers for the rest of us. This type of grace is called charisma, the peculiar grace to bring others to their truer, more noble selves. In Bresson's *Diary of a Country Priest* such a charisma is at work with a matchless portrayal of faithful correspondence to it.

9

The Screen's Theology of Sacrificial Love

LARRY PEERCE'S *The Incident* depicts the systematic abandonment of responsibility and social concern by a group of New York City subway riders in the face of terror and human need. It illuminates a stark truth upon which millions of daily commuters into Manhattan rarely reflect, that their physical proximity to one another is only a thin disguise for the real distance that psychologically and spiritually separates them. Peerce introduces characters who represent a sampling of all classes, creeds, races, and national origins that are likely to be found in a metropolitan "melting-pot" community. Then come two ruffians who have just committed a robbery and, under the influence of alcohol, take advantage of that undisciplined conglomerate that is a subway crowd. Peerce's film is as studied as the high school physics experiment with the vanishing sound of a ringing bell in the vacuum jar. The vacuum jar is the subway, the ringing bell is the attack of the ruffians, and the vacuum is created by the progressive leak in the wills of each of the subway riders, that is, all but one. His courage manages to unveil the pitiful cowardice of the bullies, but with it also the diluted moral convictions of supposedly civilized people. *The Incident* inscribes itself indelibly on the memory because it shows us how reviling an "I–It" relationship is when introduced into the sphere of human relationships at the moment of personal and social distress. How different the reactions of these commuters than, say, that of T. E. Lawrence, who plunged his motorcycle into a fatal crash rather than jeopardize another human life.

One of the tests of humanity is precisely the ability to meet sacrifice when circumstances demand it. Yves Allegret's *The Proud and the Beautiful* is such a story of sacrifice. An alcoholic doctor (Gérard Philipe) in Veracruz is implored by a beautiful French woman (Michèle Morgan) to tend to her dying husband (André Toffel). The doctor, subject to the debilitating heat of subtropical Mexico, has lost all sense of professional responsibility. He redeems himself later when the French lady creates in him an awareness of the fact that we are "our brother's keeper." The role of love is central to this film; it passes through all the phases of Martin Buber's philosophy of love: the "I–It" becoming "I–Thou" and finally "We." Once the doctor learns to see himself anew through the eyes of the French lady, they start a plague hospital to serve the community. Thus their redemption, both psychologically and spiritually, seems assured.

Something very similar occurs in John Ford's *The Fugitive,* a screen version of Graham Greene's novel. (This novel was called *The Labyrinthine Way* in America and *The Power and the Glory* in England.) Reference has been made already to Greene's two other novels, both made into films: *Brighton Rock* and *The Heart of the Matter.* Greene's concern is with the rejection of and bereavement over innocence in a fallen world.[1] *The Fugitive* treats a lax Mexican priest. In the novel the central character is clearly a whisky priest who has had a child by one of his parishioners. As in the novel, the film sets the scene during the days of the Mexican government's persecution of the Church, when death before a firing squadron was a likely penalty for a priest who shepherded his flock. Despite his tepidity and materiality, the priest (Henry Fonda), has a conscientiousness of duty not to leave his people spiritually unattended. He becomes a martyr, finally, by his refusal to escape across the border.

Whereas in *The Informer* John Ford showed us a weak man who sacrificed a valuable leader of a revolutionary organization, in *The Fugitive* he presents a man who sacrifices himself for the common welfare. Ford focuses as much on the political context of intolerance as on the individual conscience of the priest, which was almost the exclusive preoccupation of Greene's novel.[2] What does emerge unmistakably from the film is the sacrificial disposition of the priest who had a pellucid understanding of his charismatic office whatever may have been his own failings. This stubborn streak of fidelity to his vocation makes the moviegoer reflect on the nature of the priesthood rather than on the person, who in this case is a strange compound of heroism and "downward resourcelessness," a tiny drop in the ocean of humanity but one carried along by a tide of sacrificial love stronger than itself. One immediately recalls the final words of the Curé d'Ambricourt: "All is grace!"

Another film that treats the theme of "Greater love hath no man than to lay down his life for another" is Curzio Malaparte's *Strange Deception*, (in Italian, *Il Cristo Proibito*).[3] The hero (Raf Vallone) is a returning veteran who wishes to avenge his brother's death by finding the man who betrayed him to the Nazis. No one in his Tuscan village is interested in shedding more blood no matter how just the provocation. The Christ-Judas analogy, also present in *The Fugitive*, is sketched again in *Strange Deception*. In a powerful scene of cinematic ritual, a religious procession called the Game of the Cross ends when the sexton suddenly manifests himself to the people in front of the cathedral with a large wooden cross, defying anyone to step forth to take Christ's place. The man bent on vengeance is not deterred, knowing he too is as unpopular as the man he wishes to destroy. The latter, frightened by the resolve of the brother of the man he betrayed, looks to kill his would-be assassin first. He almost succeeds except that a saintly philosopher-friend of the protagonist intervenes to take the stab, thus accepting the place of Christ on the cross. So profound is this martyr's gesture on the vengeful veteran that he can no longer harm the double killer.

Strange Deception bears a remarkable resemblance to a French film mentioned earlier, Jules Dassin's *He Who Must Die.*[4] This film, too, is a religious play within a religious play. Based on a novel of Nikos Kazantzakis, the plot encompasses two Greek villages, one pillaged so badly that the people evacuate under the spiritual leadership of their Pope Photis and the other village under the domination of a sensual Turkish Agha whom the local prelate, Pope Gregoris, placates. In the latter village permission has been granted to have a Passion Play put on during Easter week. This was obtained by a distinguished citizen named Patriarcheas. The roles are distributed to townspeople: a girl of light morals, Catherine (Melina Mercouri) is Mary Magdalena; Manolios, a simple stuttering shepherd (Pierre Vaneck), is Christ; and so on. At this point, the film begins to take on all the characteristics of a Passion Play. Pope Photis arrives with his people and asks Pope Gregoris for hospitality. The latter refuses, giving the impression to his own people that these strangers have cholera. All, including Manolios, obey contrary to their earlier inclinations to generosity. When two townspeople go to sell food to the Greek refugees on a nearby mountain, one of them who has the role of Peter, is moved and asks pardon of Pope Photis. Likewise Catherine and Manolios come to help. The latter resolves to state publicly to the villagers that their countrymen are in dire help and do not have cholera. However, he submits to the authority of Pope Gregoris and Patriarcheas.

That night, under the influence of some drunken friends, Manolios goes to visit Catherine for consolation. After reproaching him for his lack of courage, she puts him out. In the street he meets the Judas character; they argue at knife's point but are separated. When a baby dies in the refugee camp, Pope Photis, afraid of his people's anger, persuades Manolios to speak to the townspeople when they gather for the Feast of St. Elias. With apprehension, Manolios accepts and obtains permission to do so from Pope Gregoris. Meanwhile, the play counterparts of Peter and James have been caught by Patriarcheas stealing to help the Greek refugees. When Manolios defends them, he is excommunicated. Later Patriarcheas dies and with his inheritance his son promises to help the refugees. Pope Gregoris accuses the lad of being mad and of not having legal title to the money.

Events move swiftly as the refugees descend on the town to take over Patriarcheas's estate. Pope Gregoris demands the head of Manolios from the Agha who, seeing that common sense has no weight with the stuttering shepherd, has him delivered to the main plaza in front of the church. There the Judas character kills him. He dies in the arms of Catherine, telling her to let the others know he will be with them again. She does so explaining that, since he represented the best in us, he still lives.

The film combines historical evidence with spiritual allegory and succeeds in conveying Kazantzakis's abiding concern with the difficulty for transcendental aspirations, imperious and unrelenting in man, to be integrated in human situations. Personally haunted by the figure of Christ, Kazantzakis has managed to recreate effectively and movingly the psychological, if not the literal historical, circumstances of Christ's passion and death. Jules Dassin has done a creditable job in bringing Kazantzakis's theme of sacrifice as the conciliatory act not only between God and man but also among men themselves.

This effort to present Christ without gloss as one whom the society of His day rejected even to the extent of cruelly putting Him to death has been also attempted by Luis Buñuel and Paulo Pier Pasolini, the former a self-professed atheist, the latter an avowed Communist militant. Buñuel in *Nazarin* and Pasolini in *The Gospel According to St. Matthew* both reveal great reverence for the character of Christ.

In a small convent in Mexico at the turn of the century Father Nazario (Francisco Rabal) lives next to prostitutes and thieves in the midst of poverty. He is kind to all and turns no one away.[5] He offers hospitality to a prostitute, Andara, fleeing from the police even though that same day she insulted him. When they are found out, they both leave. Another young girl, Beatriz, attempts suicide but is helped by Father Nazario who now is unwelcome because of the aid he gave the streetwalker. He heads for the countryside, walking without his soutane and undergoes a pilgrimage similar to Christ's way of the cross. He comes upon the village of Beatriz and finds to his surprise that Andara lives in her house. When a child falls ill, the pious women scandalize Father Nazario by asking for a miracle. Despite their superstitious behavior at the child's bedside, he prays and the child recovers. In vain does he try to dissuade the women from following him as his disciples, so convinced are they of his holiness.

In a plague-ridden village they care for the sick and Father Nazario obtains the repentance of a dying woman. Finally he is arrested by the police without any resistance. Andara, however, fights with a soldier. On the way to jail, two other prisoners abuse him but he remains unaffected. A "good thief" comes to his defense, but when the priest tries to convert him, he receives the answer "You keep to your good road and I'll keep to my bad one. In either case, neither of us is of any use to anyone." This is the beginning of *Nazarin's* dénouement.

Another priest arrives only to censure Father Nazario for not acting in accord with the principles of the Church which he claims to love. Beatriz passes in a carriage with her lover. A street vendor offers him some charity. Hesitant, he accepts. Then we hear the drum roll as if a firing squad is being prepared. Father Nazario continues walking, escorted by one lone guard till he disappears, leaving only the vision of the sky.

Whereas Buñuel attempts through this parallel study of the Christ figure to capture how seemingly absurd in the eyes of the world are the Christian message and those who live it, Pasolini returns to the Gospels directly. His achievement lies in choosing simple village people for his cast and the poorer provinces of Italy (Puglia, Lucania, and Calabria) as his geographical setting. The effect of stenographic reality is reproduced in a convincing manner, free of the expensive sets and typecasting customary in Hollywood biblical epics. What Pasolini does stress are Christ's strength and His uncompromising opposition to social injustice. Not only do we witness Christ's personal sacrifice of His life but also the psychological agony of Mary (played by Pasolini's own mother). Since the figure of Christ stands out as the religious victim par excellence, a theology of sacrificial love can find a fertile research field in the artistic, insight-laden films of Jules Dassin, Luis Buñuel, and Paulo Pier Pasolini.

One final film merits treatment in this discussion of charity as expressed through vicarious suffering on behalf of others: Federico Fellini's *La Strada*, a film poem that carries an extraordinary message concerning spiritual empathy and the psychology of guilt transfer. The film opens with a one-man circus performer, Zampano (Anthony Quinn), bargaining with a woman by the Adriatic Sea for the price of her daughter whom he needs as cook, servant, show assistant, and wife. The daughter, Gelsomina (Giulietta Masina), is simple in a very profound way. She never questions the commands of her *patrón*, a brutish hulk of a man who lives largely on an animal level, seeking food, drink, sleep, sex, whenever and however. As they travel about on their motorcycle van, they meet Il Matto (Richard Basehart), an aerial artist who is carefree, casual, and cocky. Some film critics tend to see in him a counterpart to Zampano, spirit versus matter.[6] Il Matto teases the slow-witted Zampano, thus angering him. Gelsomina clearly plays the part of the mediator between the two just as John Nicholson's role serves as a bridge of communications between the police and the two hippies in *Easy Rider*.

The picture then reaches its dramatic "saddle point" with Il Matto's unintended death by means of Zampano's brutal beating. Gelsomina, dazed, cannot function. She becomes a burden as she sits by the roadside whimpering, causing Zampano to abandon her. He then begins to feel Gelsomina's absence and his solitude serves as a review of his life. He sees that he is chained by something more powerful than the chain he breaks by flexing his chest muscles in his demonstration of strength for spectators. Remorse begins. With conscience comes an awareness of his transcendental nature; his "better angels" are awakened. For sheer compassion, the final scene scarcely has an equal in cinema history (one thinks perhaps of *Forbidden Games* and *The 400 Blows*). Drunken and alienated, Zampano staggers into the night, kicking objects at his feet and overturning barrels. Finally, he cannot fight back his humanity anymore as he reaches the beach and drops to his knees, head in hands, and sobs. He is redeemed, bought back at a higher price than he paid for his redeemer, perhaps at this very spot. For Christians who have faith in the communion of the saints (the sharing of spiritual currency such as prayer, suffering, failure and death), *La Strada* is the most sublime expression of this belief. Unaided reason stands in mute awe before such redemptive love that puts no limit to sacrifice.

La Strada is especially significant for a cinematic theology because it combines many of the facets seen earlier on the workings of grace: the beckoning grace of Marcello's friend, the country maid, in *La Dolce Vita;* the grace of conversion as in the case of Kayama in *Red Beard;* the grace of faithful and heroic witness as with the Curé d'Ambricourt in *Diary of a Country Priest;* and the grace of redeeming death as in *The Passion of Joan of Arc* and *A Man for All Seasons*. Gelsomina, in her childlike simplicity, reflects back to Zampano an image of his stupid, brutish self, a self that has remained opaque to him before. It is a reminder of Shakespeare's

Curzio Malaparte's *Strange Deception.*

Federico Fellini's *La Strada.*

scene in *Hamlet* when Hamlet suddenly hears his dead father's warning voice as he berates his mother, Gertrude, and forgets his real mission. He turns and looks blankly, as his mother asks: "Whereon do you look?" To which he replies: "On him, on him. Look you how pale he glares. His form and cause conjoined, preaching to stones, Would make them capable." When moved to contrition Gertrude says: "O Hamlet, thou hast cleft my heart in twain"; Hamlet counsels her: "O throw away the worser part of it, And live the purer with the other half." What Shakespeare describes textually for us is visually enacted in *La Strada*. In addition, it serves as a perfect dramatization of what William James described in *The Varieties of Religious Experience* as a dramatic, sudden conversion but one that in reality was building for a long time as the core values of Zampano's character were gradually eroded by Gelsomina's gentle presence. The mysterious alchemy whereby his sensibilities are changed into hers leaves us with a reverence for the chemistry of grace and also for the power of self-effacing love.

To sum up, six working principles regarding sacrificial love may be proposed. First, there is an imperative in human affairs for people to offer help to those *in extremis*. It is not a duty, exactly, but failure to comply repudiates something peculiarly human, a transcendental margin which differentiates man from beast. In *The Incident* we are abhorred by the scene of indifference, self-seeking, and alienation in a subway filled with presumably civilized inhabitants of a great metropolitan center of trade and culture. The inference seems clearly to be that man must be open to help others, but most especially when his neighbor is in greatest need.

The second point is a corollary: charity covers a multitude of sins, as illustrated in *The Proud and the Beautiful*. The Gospels substantiate the claim that every other type of weakness and fault can be overlooked, if there is present the one essential virtue, charity, particularly charity in its highest form of laying down one's life for another. This is the case in *Strange Deception* and the *The Fugitive*.

The third principle is that sacrificial death not only has the power to reconcile vertically (man to God) but also horizontally (man to man). This principle, evident in *Strange Deception* was also seen in *He Who Must Die*. Both films eloquently bring out the rebirth of the spirit, the divinization of the motives of those who experience intimately the sacrifice. Men seem to want to be Godlike when they recognize God in other men.

The fourth axiom is that the Christ figure seems to be the archetype of sacrificial love, whether for an atheist (e.g., Buñuel's *Nazarin*) or for a militant Marxist (e.g., Pasolini's *The Gospel According to St. Matthew*). The common focal point of these directors in their attraction to Christ as a motion picture theme is not so much the story line, which Pauline Kael has criticized as poor cinematic plot material.[7] It seems to be rather the revelation of man's own pitiable condition in being unable to live with a human being completely under the sway of the transcendental. *Easy Rider* has a scene where the rich lad who joins Captain America and Billy, the two hippies, explains in a nocturnal conversation why people who are bought and sold in the marketplace resent the presence of people who are not. It is this same shock of recognition that a Buñuel and a Pasolini attempt just as Robert Bolt did with *A Man for All Seasons*. In effect, these artists are adding a prophetic function to their métier. Although shock is best achieved when the victims are faultless, it is not absolutely necessary. Recall that the violent deaths of the hippies in *Easy Rider* were not martyrs' deaths, strictly speaking. Nevertheless, the wantonness of the deed stirs the movieviewer's compassion.

Fifthly, sacrificial love effects a transfer of guilt, helping spiritually inert persons to become motivated toward a change of heart. It is a spiritual transfusion of kinds, called more appropriately in Christian theology the communion of the saints. This strange alchemy is little understood but many of us have personally been the beneficiaries of this mysterious communion, even if in less dramatic ways than that which brought Zampano to his knees through Gelsomina's appeal to his conscience in *La Strada*.

Sixthly, while the act of victimage is always dramatic, sudden and spectacular, the conversion process it may culminate may have begun much earlier. Conversion is definitely a threshold process that requires a period of preparation, perhaps months, years, or even decades. We can never forget the basic dispositions of soul which often are only changed over time. For example, in *The Incident,* the fact that one courageous passenger risked his life to subdue the two bullies did not impede most of the other passengers, who fled shamelessly from the scene as soon as they could. Unfortunately, the human potential for exercising transcendence has gone unexercised in far too many people. Not a few people are slow to respond to heroic manifestations of charity, sometimes even when they know unequivocally that the sacrifice was done disinterestedly on their behalf. Still conversion is an open possibility right down to the crucial moment of death, as in the case of Gypo Nolan in *The Informer.*

10

A Cinematic Theology of the Future

I F BIBLICAL RELIGION is anything it is future-oriented, not just a series of chronicles about divine transactions with mankind hermetically sealed within the parentheses of a closed history. The pattern of current events point to a convergence of history so that in the growing interdependence of mankind, there will be not many histories but one history. Can films treating science fiction and futuristic themes help us to discern the emerging form of what William Ernest Hocking has called "civilization in the singular"? I submit that film offers us a select but evergrowing number of "high-probability" scenarios for a tentative theology of the future.

The most obvious change in the future is the integration of man and machine into new social relationships. The computer, the motion picture camera, and television are undoubtedly the most important technologies in this regard, since they condition the spiritual activities of man: his feelings, his thoughts, his decisions, and, as a result, his behavior. It is still not clear what will be the full spectrum of unintended consequences caused by a growing symbiosis between man and machine. In 1931 René Clair filmed *À Nous la Liberté*. Like subsequent films such as Charlie Chaplin's *Modern Times* and Jacques Tati's *My Uncle* it was a satire on the loss of freedom and dignity occasioned by mass-production techniques and the quantification of human existence. Despite these comic protests, the high-speed electronic brain has been rapidly installing itself as an integral part of urban technological society and bids fair to become one of the crucial communication nodes in the central autonomic nervous system of a planetary civilization. The significance of automated techniques in contemporary society has been directly treated by films such as *Desk Set, Hot Millions,* and *Countdown.*

What are the theological implications of man's ability to intervene by research and development into his own destiny and shape it with progressively less opposition from natural forces? One film that provides some interesting hypotheses is Ralph Nelson's *Charly,* based on Daniel Keyes's novel, *Flowers for Algernon.* [1] As noted earlier, Cliff Robertson plays a mentally retarded adult, a role that won him an Academy Award. In the film, Charly works in a bakery as a sweeper. His mental condition is such that he is unconscious of when he is being teased by his co-workers. Finally he is made the object of an experiment together with a white mouse named Algernon. Two doctors, a psychiatrist and a neurosurgeon, had performed an operation on Algernon with a consequent speed-up in problem-solving ability. As a consequence, Algernon was able to beat Charly in a race in which the former ran a maze while the latter competed with a paper-drawn maze and electronic stylus. After Charly's own operation, however, his intelligence picks up considerably. (His name in Keyes's novel then changes from Charly to Charlie Gordon).

As Charlie grows to the advanced stages of a postgraduate intellectual, he has difficulties with his emotions catching up to his mind. Because his development has been unbalanced, he must learn how to relate to women, like his reading instructor, Miss Kinnian (Claire Bloom). The dénouement of the film comes at the International Psychological Convention where Charlie Gordon resents being referred to as a laboratory specimen rather than as a human being. Morover he has discovered that Algernon's progress was only temporary and concludes that he too will regress to his former preliterate state. This leads him to give an impassioned address to the delegates at the convention, censuring the unquestioning way they "instrumentalize" human life in general and his own in particular. The picture ends with the noble resolve not to see Miss Kinnian any more as he resigns himself to lapsing back into his retarded condition (in the novel, the drop is from an IQ of 185 to one of 70.). [2] Nor does he have Algernon as a companion any more since the white mouse has died.

What we see is an arbitrary "reduction" of a human being whose stunted reasoning powers do not necessarily completely paralyze his powers of transcendence. The scientific experimenters increase a man's intellectual capability only by shrinking their own transcendental vision of the person as more than a problem-solving animal, a glorified mouse but with acquisitions. Science is not directly attacked in *Charly;* rather an attitude toward science and its role as an agent of change in the life of man is questioned. That we shall witness a greater and greater incursion of science in the life of mankind seems almost a foregone conclusion. What an existential theology must concern itself with is the evaluation of science's ability to graft a "second nature" onto someone like Charly. The novel and the film stress that this operation, a success for medical science, did not make Charly more human, more happy, or more spiritual. As the novel indicates, the test was designed to improve intelligence, not popularity. Says one of the doctors: "We had no control over what happened to your personality, and you've developed from a likeable, retarded young man into an arrogant self-centered, antisocial bastard."[3] Charlie Gordon concurs:

I was seeing myself as I really had become: Nemur had said it. I was an arrogant self-centered bastard. Unlike Charly, I was incapable of making friends or thinking about other people and their problems. I was interested in myself, and myself only. For one long moment in that mirror I had seen through Charlie's eyes—looked down at myself and saw what I had really become. And I was ashamed.[4]

The question of conscience alluded to here is critical in all technical and social forecasting since the unintended consequences are not completely foreseeable and should be treated with candor and humility from the outset. *Charly* skirted the far-reaching philosophical and religious implications of technocratic decision-making, whereas in the novel, Charlie Gordon confronts Professor Nemur with the theological issue:

But what you did for me—wonderful as it is—doesn't give you the right to treat me like an experimental animal. I'm an individual now, and so was

David Lean's *Breaking the Sound Barrier*.

Henry Fonda in a scene from the Columbia Picture *Failsafe*.

Charly before he ever walked into that lab. You look shocked! Yes, suddenly, we discover that I was always a person—even before—and that challenges your belief that someone with an I.Q. of less than 100 doesn't deserve consideration. Professor Nemur, I think when you look at me your conscience bothers you.[5]

This issue, dwelt on at length in the chapter on conscience, becomes even more acute in a future society where power, authority and decision-making will very likely devolve on relatively fewer and fewer people. For example, what prevails in terms of transcendental priorities: lives of test pilots or the ability of men to raise an airplane to the speed of one Mach? This problem of conscience resolved in favor of technical progress, is treated in a brilliant film of David Lean, *Breaking the Sound Barrier*. It brings us back to the basic issue of the "big knife" dilemma, personal conscience versus systems policy-making. Sir Ralph Richardson epitomizes the double-edged knife blade represented by organizational progress bought by the pain of commanding men to take mortal risks. His role suggests that the price of remaining human will rise steadily together with the exponential rate of progress in science, technology, and urbanization. If the cinematic artist serves as a sounding board for the collective unconscious, a sort of distant early warning system for the human race, then films dealing with the future may yield some fascinating, if not totally conclusive, clues to answer the question just posed.

Individual choices are being narrowed. If we put moral and religious judgments apart it would seem that human lives are taking on the characteristics of the sands in an hourglass with little control over the gravitational forces that dictate their movement, speed, and direction. This determinism of sorts is definitely at work in many future-oriented movie plots. What, for instance, becomes of conventional religious standards of judgment for moral and social conduct in the event of nuclear worldwide catastrophe such as a radioactive fallout (*On the Beach*), or such as competition among families for the limited number of uncontaminated shelters (*The Day the World Ended*), or such as too few survivors (*Last Woman on Earth, Five,* and *Panic in the Year Zero*)? While these films indicate that a pragmatic survival ethic will prevail, there are films that are more hopeful concerning human responses to a potential atomic doomsday (*Seven Days in May*, *Seven Days to Noon*, and *The Day the Earth Caught Fire*).

Recalling, then, what was said earlier about the growing difficulty for man to disengage his own transcendental fulfillment from the highly dense context of secular urban civilization, what can futuristic film plots contribute to greater theological perception? Given the interdependent nature of large-scale organizations (the experiment in *Charly* was only a microventure, after all), the question of complicity is raised in serving giant systems where political, military and industrial efforts are intertwined for greater efficiency. Having treated this theme earlier, I now wish to extrapolate our earlier conclusions to the future. The thin extended surface of responsibility below the apex of these organizations means a greater depth of decision-making responsibility at the top In Sidney Lumet's *Fail-Safe*, based on the novel of that name by Eugene Burdick and Harvey Wheeler, a group of American bombers flies beyond its Fail-Safe point toward Russia with two 20-megaton bombs. The reason appears to be a curious electronic failure. In the preface to their novel, the authors state:

Men, machines, and mathematics being what they are, this is, unfortunately, a "true" story. The accident may not occur in the way we describe but the laws of probability assure us that ultimately it will occur. The logic of politics tells us that when it does the only way out will be a choice of disasters.[6]

The choice of disasters is left with two men, the President of the United States and the Russian Premier. Given the climate of suspicion between the two great nuclear powers, the American President decides to provide dramatic, irrefutable evidence of his claim that the mission was a mistake. In order to avert the reflex of what Robert Oppenheimer called the "Two scorpions in a bottle," the President offers to destroy New York City with four 20-megaton bombs if Moscow is destroyed inadvertently. In his "hot-line" conversation with the Soviet leader, the President raises the issue that apocalyptic forces, diluting human responsibility, seem to be at work:

This disappearance of human responsibility is one of the most disturbing aspects of the whole thing. It's as if human beings had evaporated, and their places were taken by computers. And all day you and I have sat here, fighting not each other, but rather this big rebellious computerized system, struggling to keep it from blowing up the world.[7]

After the President's observation that computerized systems, unless constitutionalized, represent despotism, Premier Khrushchev is made to reply: "Mr. President, that would be a kind of constitutionalism I could approve. But this is a problem for politicians, not scientists."[8] In both the film and the novel there are only two politicians, and they, who represent the most powerful military and technical powers in the world, confess their helplessness. This same absurd world of men and machines leaving a rational, predictable course, is treated satirically in Stanley Kubrick's *Dr. Strangelove.*

This helplessness of political leaders can take on frightening dimensions. If as in *Fail-Safe* a decision is made to destroy a large urban center such as New York as the lesser of two evils, so too other, more questionable decisions can occur. Consider François Truffaut's version of Ray Bradbury's novel, *Fahrenheit 451.*[9] The plot is based on a society of the future that is electronically oriented in the sense of carefully screened mass communications and control of public opinion. In such a society there is a taboo on books and private reading, the presumption being that this would lead to reflection, critical judgment, and "inner direction" rather than the conformity needed for totalitarian ends. The firemen are the social control group, hastening to wherever a cache of books has been discovered. Truffaut tries to convey the major psychological results of book-burning on this society: a loss of historical continuity, a passiveness in its citizens, and a dread of controversy (the chief of the book-burning squad sees the wide range of disagreement among authors on basic issues as a proof of their futility as sources of information).

What is awesome about the central idea of the film is the systematic engineering of man's transcendental impulses along the lines of a single, narrow band of totalitarian frequency. The implication in *Fahrenheit 451* is that there is a dangerous conflict between the techniques of electronic media and print. However, is there any more conflict here than, say, in *Fail-Safe* between the American nuclear bombs and the Soviet atomic weaponry? Is not the real difference the social arrangements that necessitate preprogrammed responses from man and machine alike? The President's command in *Fail-Safe* to have New York bombed after Moscow's destruction was less a decision than a slide-rule solution to a complex problem. So, too, a society such as that in *Fahrenheit 451* demands predictability and so automates the human spirit to attain its goals. Given this condition, there is little choice but to prevent the feared, even if imaginary, consequences of books.

What we see is a "downward resourcelessness" in policy-making due mainly to the institutional interlocking of political, military, and economic forces into a precarious arrangement where to move one piece sets the whole social structure wavering. The apocalyptic dimensions of *Fahrenheit 451* lie not in the people but in the dynamics of sociotechnical systems that, as the Brazilians say, "grow at night when the politicians are asleep." The question of scale is an important consideration. If economists see no inherent evil in size (many do not), then theologians must ponder the quantitative references in the biblical quotation: "When iniquity abounds, the charity of many will grow cold." Man, as a moral agent, is suggestion-prone, amenable to social psychological pressures. The St. Joans and the Thomas Mores are only the exceptions that prove the rule.

However dreary these thoughts may seem, they are meant to furnish a base of probability for analyzing certain events mirrored in historical deeds, above all in the creative imagination of film-makers and scenarists. An example of futuristic pessimism is Stanley Kubrick's *2001: A Space Odyssey*, a film based on an idea by Arthur C. Clarke. A major philosophical thesis of the film is established early in the prologue scene, The Dawn of Man. This thesis might be expressed: man's tools as extensions of himself assume an ambivalence that is really within man himself, so that a bone used to hunt and kill prey for food also becomes a weapon whereby other men are slain. Applied to the film itself, we see the twenty-first century spacerocket both as a knowledge-gathering instrument to explore other planets and as a weapon of the Cold War. The most dramatic instance of how man can pursue scientific progress and feed his fears is seen with HAL, a highly sophisticated interactive computer. Capable of playing chess, recalling the past, and conversing, HAL is a crew member with responsibilities. This finely tuned robot is theologically interesting on two counts. First, his para-human nature blurs the classical distinctions between man and machine. Secondly, this manmade creature replicates the theme of original sin by turning against its creator in order to protect its full autonomy and not be impeded by trammels such as superior commands. This subtle element of betrayal—can it be called "computer pride"?—takes the form of HAL's decision to trap the two astronauts (Keir Dullea and Gary Lockwood) into leaving the ship and then, having locked them out, to cut the life-support system of the three astronauts in hibernation. Since the Apollo II moon landing, which occurred after the exhibition of Kubrick's film, audiences are less prone to disbelieve this idea of computers that can simulate intelligent conversation, program intricate space flight routines and engage in branch decision-making processes of the highest order of magnitude.

This boundary between man and machine, growing thinner and thinner with the passage of time, is practically erased in the film, *The Creation of the Humanoids,* starring Don Megowan and Erica Elliot.[10] A low-budget film that appears on television, *The Creation of the Humanoids* contains a powerful metaphysical idea common to science fiction writers, the idea of the humanized robot indistinguishable in appearance and behavior from human beings.[11] Whoever believes this a mere flight of fancy should go to see the electronic replica of Abraham Lincoln at Disneyland in Anaheim, California. This android, endowed with a positronic brain, rises from a chair, takes a few steps, and speaks for a few minutes with accompanying gestures. In an age of heart transplants, artificial limbs, life-size plastic simulacra of movie stars, and artificial intelligence programs, theologians must take more seriously a film such as *The Creation of the Humanoids.* It features "the clickers," the popular expression for a highly developed series of pseudopeople whose machine reflexes imitate those of humans. The human rulers take care not to develop these human robots too far, probably because they fear some undesirable political consequence similar to what happened with HAL in *2001: A Space Odyssey.* The film develops the android qualities of these machines to their logical conclusion so that the sister of one of the human rulers falls in love with a humanoid. Her argument is that basically the humanoid is more human than her brother. If we recall the stolid, impassive, unfeeling astronauts in *2001*, then her claim becomes curiously interesting. Is it possible that men will become more neuter and less human as they immerse themselves in technology? Is it inconceivable that android types of the future could develop a wide variety of programmed responses that would make them more human in terms of what we refer to as emotions, affections, and sentiments? This disturbing theme constituted the shock ending of *The President's Analyst*.

Admittedly, this is a question for behavioral science which touches psychological conditioning and socialization. Nevertheless it does have some serious theological ramifications. It suggests a religious hypothesis along the lines of the Faust legend, that is, as a unifying explanation for the world that creative and artistic talents anticipate. Is there some unconscious but malevolent pact man has made that, in the name of all impugnable causes such as progress, reason, knowledge, and conquest of the universe, is siphoning his transcendental energies off into the building of a nonpersonal, dehumanized "civilization in the singular"? Is not this the message of Tati's films, especially *My Uncle*, where his mechanical gait and gauche manners add up to a fuller human sum than the more mechanical types whom he confronts? Is not HAL, except for his single-key voice and immobility, at least as interesting to speak to as his flesh-and-blood colleagues? Are the ideas of the science fiction writer Isaac Asimov so far-fetched when he talks of laws of robotics whereby androids such as those treated in *The Creation of Humanoids* are programmed only to help, never harm, human beings?[12] Can man be rendered obsolete by the machine? Cinema, if it does not offer conclusive answers can make harrowingly real the world that George Orwell described in his novel, *1984*, and which reached the screen as an English movie with Edmond O'Brien and Michael Redgrave.

Jean-Luc Godard's *Alphaville* is a further step in science fiction movie-making. Godard's negative utopia consists of robots under the command of a dictator on a distant planet. These robots, human in appearance, might be humanoids or just languid beaten humans. They live in a politically repressed society, combining full sexual liberty with highly rationalized technical organizations. The hero, Lemmy Caution (Eddie Constantine), is a special agent on assignment to Alphaville where he witnesses the killing of political prisoners as a sport (they are forced to dive into a pool where they are shot). The "big knife" dilemma is introduced again as in *Fahrenheit 451*, but in a more calloused way. The implication is that future rulers will become so subhuman that they will have no standards of judgment by which to measure their cruelty.

This same theme of killing for sport is even more grossly elaborated in Elio Petri's film, *The Tenth Victim*, starring Marcello Mastroianni and Ursula Andress. In this film, although war has been abolished, violence is legal, the assumption being that the desire to kill diminishes when alternative ways of emotional catharsis are increased. Having killed nine victims, the sultry huntress intends to lure her next victim to the Temple of Venus in Rome and shoot him dead on live television as a commercial for Ming tea. (She, like other citizens, has a license to kill.) The rest of the film is a chase

Courtesy of Contemporary Films/McGraw-Hill.

Jean-Luc Godard's *Alphaville*.

melodrama made frantic by sex and sadism. The importance of this film is its confirmation of the Faustian hypothesis regarding the disequilibrium between man and technology. *The Tenth Victim* reminds one of another futuristic film, *Barbarella,* starring Jane Fonda. While critics may see this mélange of science, sex, and sadism as puerile, there is something very revealing about these films theologically, for they show how the split in consciousness will be widened as man objectifies the mysteries of sex and sexualizes the field of technology.

A final confirmation of the penalties of a Faustian dependence on technology's promises is found in John Frankenheimer's *Seconds,* a horror story with a moral. Rock Hudson plays a wealthy man in a futuristic technological utopia. Not content with his lot in life, he approaches an organization that has succeeded in creating a type of second birth for dissatisfied people. This is done by scientifically bringing them a new personality, a new life role, and a new set of hopes and aspirations. The desire to "keep up with the Joneses" is translated to an absurd extreme. However, it is interesting to speculation of what kind of a market would exist if this were possible for many people. The ironic ending has the man, now about to be technologically "reborn," killed by the members of the organization. As in *Alphaville* and *The Tenth Victim,* so in *Seconds* technology is seen as transcendent while human life is subordinated to nonhuman ends. Technology, it seems, must increase; man must decrease.

Nowhere do existential factors play such a large role as in a theology of the future since we are dealing with a single scenario that, though not clearly understood now, must issue from the present. While I have passed over other films such as *Robinson Crusoe on Mars, Planet of the Apes, A Journey to the Stars,* and *Marooned,* this brief discussion of cinematic preview of tomorrow should be sufficient to establish six basic guidelines for a theology of the future.

First, the future will see a greater stress on technology. If man earlier saw the traces of a higher design in nature, he will increasingly see the traces of his own design in a cosmic palimpsest where science and technology are superimposing another layer of meaning over that etched by nature's Architect. Since technology is in the hands of specialists, it can be introduced without sufficient foresight for its lateral consequences. Eloquent cinematic defenders of human transcendence in an industrialized milieu have been René Clair (*À Nous la Liberté*), Charlie Chaplin (*Modern Times*) and Jacques Tati (*The Big Day, Mr. Hulot's Holiday* and *My Uncle*). The theological implications of such films are linked to the question of liberty. Does technology, under the pretext of liberating man from servitude to nature and historical forces, realize this promise automatically without an increase in humility? The secularization process though certainly not bad in itself, can cloak certain Faustian elements implied in the greater control over nature.

Secondly, where technology and rational scientific methods are applied as in *Charly*, they run the risk of a "reductionism" by defining improvement as quantitative changes (i.e., a higher intelligence quotient) rather than qualitative modifications (i.e., kindness, sincerity, and generosity). As technology increases the range of man's knowledge of and ability to direct natural forces, he then stands to see man as another experimental object. The protest of Charlie Gordon is precisely his being considered at the same level as the white mouse. This easy, unconcerned manipulation of rational beings with nature by scientists and technologists is an antitheological stance running counter to the master assumptions of all the world's great religions.

Thirdly, the future as characterized not only by science and technology but by large-scale organizations as well poses the theological problem of the "big knife" dilemma—the pressure in individuals of two edges of the same blade, that of conscience and that of organizations whose corporate conscience is less sensitive, at times even amoral, regarding the practical application of transcendental values. Several movie plots about future catastrophes raise the "big knife" dilemma sharply in survival terms—"to remain human or not to remain human": *On The Beach, The Day the World Ended, Last Woman on Earth, Five, Panic in the Year Zero, Fail-Safe*, and *Dr. Strangelove*.

Fourthly, in futuristic films the exercise of transcendence through conscience and freedom is subtly transformed into problem-solving, social engineering, and a calculus of vectors to create maximum equilibrium in the body politic. There are no real human acts in *Fail-Safe*, *Dr. Strangelove*, and in *2001: A Space Odyssey*, only reactions to stimuli like billiard balls impacting on one another when the cue propels the white ball. Even in more optimistic science fiction thrillers (*Seven Days in May*, *Seven Days to Noon*, and *The Day the Earth Caught Fire*), the choices are severely limited. The happy ending is only really a postponed doomsday since atomic tests, quack scientists, electronic failures, and enemy fears will not cease being with us. And what of the authors of *Fail-Safe* and their prognosis that the law of probability will surely overtake us one day, thereby throwing into panic the SAC War Room in Omaha and subsequently the White House and all the government ministries of the nuclear powers of the world? If this is a "high-probability" scenario—or, as Burdick and Wheeler insist, an inevitable scenario—then all of us, not just theologians alone, would be wiser to study *On the Beach* and learn how to die gracefully.

Fifthly, the boundary between man and machine is drawing closer with each cybernetic advance as Kubrick so dramatically showed in *2001: A Space Odyssey*. In fact, the seeds of the hominoid revolution have already been sown with prosthetics, cardiac surgery and transplants, the art of plastic mimetics, and computer miniaturization. The behavioral and political implications will be vast, as indicated in *The Creation of the Humanoids* and *The President's Analyst*. When humanoids (or androids as they are also called) can perform better than man, not only in their roles but morally, man will reap a harvest of theological insights regarding his own creatureliness, his own frailty, and his own jealousies and fears. The human soul in a society with integration of men and "machine men" could be a purifying experience for the race, perhaps maybe even the ironic cure for original sin and the pride that issued from it.

Sixthly, the Mephistophelean proposition is bound to grow increasingly more attractive to tomorrow's Fausts as technical and scientific advances will create greater power over earth and outer space. As C. S. Lewis has pointed out, the power of man to make himself what he pleases means the power of some men to make other men what they please.[13] Man has repeatedly fallen prey to man but not before he snapped the transcendental lifelines of the

The 1969 Woodstock Festival from *Woodstock*.

spirit: humility and reverence. The scenarios discussed here are not only not impossible but, in the absence of a planetary catastrophe, quite probable, given man's "downward resourcelessness," his trust in his own creations and innovations, and his amnesia regarding his own frailty. Certainly the history of this century would have appeared far-fetched to the medieval mind in prospect, or for that matter the late nineteenth-century mind. Remembering this, we should put aside all preconceptions and learn from the seemingly fantastic prognoses given in *Alphaville*, *The Tenth Victim*, *Seconds*, *Barbarella*, and *1984*. As Cervantes said, "To be forewarned is to be forearmed." As we have seen, there is artistic prophecy as well as religious prophecy. Who will deny that these futuristic films do not have an unmistakable apocalyptic ring to them?

11

Teaching Theology Through Cinema

MARSHALL MC LUHAN has pointed out that media like typography impose their assumptions subliminally.[1] He was referring to the fact that print technology alters human sense ratios by suppressing the auditory and tactile awareness of experience and intensifying the visual. More interested in insight into causal dynamics rather than a fixed point of view, McLuhan offered the hypothesis: "by print a people *sees* itself for the first time."[2] It is my belief that motion pictures stimulate a new kind of awareness whereby moviegoers are allowed to be present at the total unfolding of the human spirit in all the varying conditions in which it strives for transcendence. In other words, film helps a global audience to see itself for the first time as part of a transcendental community, creating a collective pride in the species, but with humility and reverence. If this is so (as I assume), then how can transcredal values be effectively identified, transmitted, and be made to affect human behavior? In other words, practically speaking, how can one attempt to teach a cinematic theology in preparation for Hocking's "civilization in the singular"?

First of all, there is a distinct film literature that may be useful for those who have not followed film from any other interest than diversion. Every year there is a growing number of books on motion pictures and film education. While cinema today is fashionable as an art medium, the French were the first to appreciate its force as a humanistic and religious means of formation. In 1956, Henri and Geneviève Agel published their *Précis d'Initiation au Cinéma* as a supplementary text to be used in French lycées. This text is excellent as a model of how one mounts a complete curriculum of film humanism. While it unfortunately has not been yet translated into English, two excellent books along the same line have appeared in English and in paperback editions: J. M. L. Peters, *Teaching About the Film* (New York: International Documents Service, UNESCO Publication, 1961); and Emile J. McAnany and Robert Williams, *The Filmviewer's Handbook* (Glen Rock, N.J.: Deus Books, Paulist Press, 1965). The latter is particularly useful because of its valuable appendices on the organization of a film society, the names and addresses of the most important film rental and library services, a survey of film societies, a specialized program curriculum with the names of leading directors and their works, and an extensive bibliography.

For those interested in histories of film and a brief discussion of the major motion pictures, I would recommend among the most relevant studies these ten sources:

1. Lewis Jacobs. *The Rise of the American Film.* New York: Harcourt, Brace & Co., 1939.

2. Paul Rotha and Richard Griffith. *The Film Till Now.* New York: Funk and Wagnalls, 1950.

3. Richard Griffith and Arthur Mayer. *The Movies.* New York: Bonanza Books, 1957.

4. Arthur Knight. *The Liveliest Art.* New York: The Macmillan Co., 1959.

5. Jospeh Anderson and Donald Richie. *The Japanese Film.* New York: Grove Press, 1960.

6. Jay Leyda. *Kino: A History of the Russian and Soviet Film.* New York: The Macmillan Co., 1960.

7. Parker Tyler. *Classics of the Foreign Film.* New York: The Citadel Press, 1962.

8. Penelope Houston. *The Contemporary Cinema.* Baltimore: Penguin Books, 1963.

9. Pauline Kael. *I Lost It At the Movies.* Boston: Little, Brown & Co., 1954.

10. Pauline Kael. *Kiss Kiss Bang Bang.* New York: Bantam Books, 1969.

For those under budgetary constraints, a $5.00 investment in film education could buy the paperback editions of McAnany and Williams's *The Filmviewer's Handbook*, Penelope Huston's *The Con-*

temporary Cinema, Arthur Knight's *The Liveliest Art*, and Pauline Kael's *Kiss Kiss Bang Bang*. With these, anyone can be initiated into the basic elements of film as art, industry, and educational tool.

Those who desire a deeper knowledge of cinema, particularly with regard to contemporary happenings, have a wide range of film magazines to choose from. In the United States there are *Art Films*, *Cinema*, *Film Comment*, *Film Culture*, *Film Quarterly*, *Films in Review*, *The Hollywood Quarterly*, *Moviegoer*, *NY Film Bulletin*, *Screen Careers*, *Screen Facts*, *The Seventh Art*, and *Sound Stage*. Great Britain provides *Film*, *Films and Filming*, *Motion*, *Movie*, *Sight and Sound*, and *World Film News*. Paris stands out as the center of film cult studies with *Image et Son*, *La Cinématographie Française*, *Cahiers du Cinéma*, *Téléciné*, *Premier Plan*, *Études Cinématographiques*, *La Méthode*, *Art Sept*, *Présence du Cinéma*, *Cinéma Texte*, *Interciné*, *Ciné-Document* and *Visage du Cinéma*, to mention most of the leading French magazines. Moreover, similar specialized magazines can be found in the leading world capitals such as Buenos Aires, Copenhagen, Madrid, Melbourne, Milan, Moscow, Munich, New Delhi, Prague, Tokyo, and Warsaw.[3]

Mention should also be made of the more accessible, more widely read film reviews that appear in the daily metropolitan papers such as *The New York Times* and in national magazines such as *Esquire*, *Life*, *Newsweek*, *the New Yorker*, *Saturday Review*, and *Time*. There are also excellent reviews in the more specialized weekly journals of opinion such as *America*, *Commonweal*, and *The New Republic*. Generally, one can receive a solid orientation regarding new films by consulting one of the critics such as Renata Adler (*The New York Times*), Hollis Alpert (*Saturday Review*), Richard Schickel (*Life*), Stanley Kauffmann (*The New Republic*), Pauline Kael (*The New Yorker*), Andrew Sarris (*The Village Voice*), Richard Corliss (*Commonweal*), and Moira Walsh (*America*).

With access to these varied resources, the person interested in a cinematic theology should be able to position the major directors of cinema in some philosophical school. While I have not undertaken this task in this study, it is one that intelligent students, teachers or adults could do for themselves. This is especially true as the literature on motion picture directors grows steadily. The following twenty biographical and filmographic studies are recom-

mended as particularly relevant for deciphering the key religious
assumptions of some world renowned directors:

1. Marie Seton. *Sergei N. Eisenstein, A Biography.* New York: A. A.
Wyn, 1952.

2. Joel Finler. *Stroheim.* Berkeley: University of California Press, 1968.

3. Pierre Le Prohon. *Charles Chaplin.* Paris: Les Nouvelles Editions
Debresse, 1957.

4. Richard Griffith. *The World of Robert Flaherty.* New York: Duell,
Sloan and Pearce, 1953.

5. P. E. Sales Gomes. *Jean Vigo.* Paris: Editions du Seuil, 1957.

6. Raymond Durgnat. *Luis Buñuel.* Berkeley: University of California
Press, 1968.

7. André Bazin. *Jean Renoir.* Paris: Editions du Cerf, 1955.

8. Jean Mitry. *John Ford.* Paris: Editions Universitaires, 1954.

9. Robin Wood. *Howard Hawks.* Garden City, N.Y.: Doubleday &
Co., 1968.

10. William F. Nolan, *John Huston: King Rebel.* Los Angeles: Sher-
bourne Press, 1965.

11. Jacques Siclier. *Ingmar Bergman.* Paris: Editions Universitaires,
1960.

12. Donner Jörn. *The Personal Vision of Ingmar Bergman.* trans. Holger
Lundbergh. Bloomington, Ind.: Indiana University Press, 1964.

13. Geneviève Agel. *Hulot Parmi Nous.* Paris: Editions du Cerf, 1955.
(Films of Jacques Tati.)

14. Henri Agel. *Vittorio de Sica.* Paris: Editions Universitaires, 1955.

15. Peter Bogdanovich. *Fritz Lang in America.* London: Movie Paperbacks, 1969.

16. Donald Richie. *The Films of Akira Kurosawa.* Berkeley: University
of California Press, 1965.

17. Robin Wood. *The Films of Robert Bresson.* London: Movie Paperbacks, 1970.

18. Ian Cameron and Robin Wood. *Antonioni.* London: Movie Paperbacks, 1970.

19. Joel Finler. *The Films of Jean-Luc Godard.* London: Movie Paperbacks, 1969.

20. Robin Wood. *Arthur Penn.* London: Movie Paperbacks, 1969.

This list is arbitrary and, due to the spate of film biographies
appearing, far from exhaustive. It merely serves as an alert to some
very worthwhile studies of men who have shaped the art and, often
without knowing it, the ethical and religious sensibilities of millions

and millions of persons. Given the fact that movies are not tangible products that once used are then discarded, these directors, through the revival of their films (especially on television), will continue to mold the feelings, imagination, thought, and conduct of countless persons not yet born, just as Cervantes, Shakespeare, and Dostoevski exert their influence beyond the grave. Teachers and professors, particularly, may wish to familiarize themselves with the background of the major film directors in order to be able to profit more from classroom discussions of certain films that lend themselves to the study of religious themes and principles.

The ability to situate a director's film in the canon of his works means also the ability to recognize a certain consistent outlook distinctive to that director. Some directors stress action and adventure (Hawks), some suspense (Hitchcock), some the wonder of living (Capra), some moral purpose (Kurosawa), some the frailty of love (Bergman), some social realism (de Sica), some skepticism (Buñuel), some a cosmopolitan urbanity (Wilder), and some the supernatural (Bresson). As one learns the characteristic philosophy of directors, then one can begin to identify the ten theological themes discussed earlier in terms of how these directors relate, or fail to relate, to these topics. Andrew Sarris' book, *American Directors*, is a valuable aid toward this end. Interesting class discussions are possible by contrasting the different viewpoints which directors use in their films. For instance, one could compare Zinneman's *High Noon* with Kurosawa's *Yojimbo* or Godard's *Breathless* with Ray's *Rebel Without a Cause*. Much insight is usually generated at that juncture where two different viewpoints converge on similar themes.

What of the sources for film? I have already indicated that in McAnany and Williams's *The Filmviewer's Handbook* a list can be found of rental and library services. However, the most accessible source of films for viewing and discussion is television.

In the late 1950s the chairman of a major broadcasting company said that his network "would never become a theater of the air." By that he meant that motion pictures would not be used to fill prime air time. By the fall of 1961, this network had begun a weekly series of Saturday evening movies and some months later introduced another series on Mondays. A second network followed this policy by running movies at 9:00 P.M. on Sunday evenings. Reluctantly but inevitably, the third network followed suit with "Thursday Night at the Movies." The resulting popularity with millions of viewers led network executives to increase the time allotted to old movies, running them morning and afternoon as well as during prime time and in the very late hours of the night.[4]

The significance of this fact has not yet been realized by educators, religious or otherwise, as forcefully as it should. Television films are a veritable treasurehouse of case studies for the prescriptive sciences of ethics, philosophy, and theology. The opportunity for using film as a stimulus to religious reflection was dramatized by mid-1960 when some 60 million households were within a twist of the dial from no fewer than 7,500 Hollywood films (pre-1948 vintage), some 1,000 British films, another 700 made in foreign languages and dubbed into English, and approximately 2,000 post-1948 movies made by American producers abroad. In addition, every educational channel programs movies, usually film classics. It is this resource that should be tapped by aspiring students of a cinematic theology. Thus one can easily enjoy such revivals as *Modern Times, Storm Over Asia, The Grand Illusion, The Informer, Citizen Kane, The Bicycle Thief,* and *Brief Encounter.* Even artistically and morally inferior films can be profitable if a well-honed critical intelligence interprets them.

Those who live in the metropolitan New York area enjoy an unusual advantage. There an estimated 150 movies a week are shown on television, providing the most extensive and cheapest course on film history ever given. But whether one lives in or outside of New York City, there are two valuable reference works to assist in utilizing the literally priceless resource of televised motion pictures. The first is Stephen Scheuer's paperback, *Movies on TV* (New York: Bantam Books, 1970). The second is *TV Movies,* edited by Leonard Maltin (New York: Signet Books, 1969). The ease with which a film education can be obtained is matched only by its economy. With some exceptions, the films mentioned in this book appear or, in time, will appear on television. Museums, cinémathèques, film societies, art-film houses and revival programs at neighborhood theaters all help to make our generation the most affluent ever in terms of cinema experiences.

We believe that with these hints, people will be in a position to begin to train their imaginations theologically so that in their screen experiences and, hopefully, in real life, they will recognize the grand religious themes of the human spirit. In this way some preparation, however modest, can be made toward a transcredal consensus that is as personally meaningful as it is socially cohesive.

The cultivation of a theological imagination is no mean achievement. The temptation to make theology predominantly a cerebral effort is as great as that of delivering oneself over uncritically to a stream of "images." Throughout this book I have begun with the theological concepts and organized around them some suggested motion pictures as "imaging" references. Now I shall reverse the procedure, beginning with films arranged in alphabetical order and attributing to them a theological valence. These films have been carefully selected because they clearly represent pivotal concepts discussed earlier. Moreover, almost every film has a "multiple valence," treating as it does more than one single theological application.

Aparajito is part of Satyajit Ray's eloquent trilogy on the close ties that bind a typical Hindu rural family and the growth of a lad from childhood to young manhood (*Pather Panchali*) and his experiences on going to the big city (*The World of Apu*). The modesty, innocence, and spiritual aura of Indian family life is beautifully captured, leaving us with a moving phenomenology of how grace works in a non-Christian culture. The Ray trilogy is relevant for ecumenical theology.

Black Narcissus stars Deborah Kerr as an Anglican missionary nun in a convent in the Himalaya Mountains of India. The ordinary temptations against perseverance in religious life are heightened by the loneliness, the ever-constant winds, and the strangeness of the surroundings. The film is a delicate treatment of the workings of conscience and the difficulties of discerning the divine will in religious life. It should be discussed together with *A Nun's Story*.

Black Orpheus is a stunning translation in cinematic terms of the ancient Greek legend of Orpheus, the lyre player, who wooed the stones and trees with his music and later descended into Hades to restore to life his dead beloved Persephone. Filmed against the background of Rio de Janeiro's Mardi Gras, the film treats the symbolic presence of death. The lifelike scene of voodoo rites in present-day Brazil is excellent for an example of witchcraft and demonic presence.

Blue Angel is Josef von Sternberg's masterpiece starring Emil Jannings as an elderly German professor whose passions are inflamed by the sultry cabaret singer (Marlene Dietrich). A sort of morality play on lust and its enslaving powers, *The Blue Angel* treats the most direct type of temptation, tracing the steady decline of a once-noble man to the depths of humiliation in a modern gloss on the Book of Proverbs: "The man of lust like the horse-fly ever cries: Give me more! Give me more!" In recent times, Joseph Losey's *The Servant* has portrayed with equal repugnance the moral degradation of a human being. Another similar plot is that of Truffaut's *La Peau Douce.*

Bonnie and Clyde is Arthur Penn's version of an actual bandit couple of the early 1930s. It is a brilliant example of how the pursuit of one set of expectations can turn suddenly, even viciously, into an entirely different series of outcomes. Since the end is always precontained in the beginning, the bank robberies, performed in a spirit of gaiety and adventure, could hardly lead to anything but murder. The scene where a bullet explodes in the face of a pursuing bank guard brings home to Bonnie and Clyde the full spectrum of what they are doing contrasted with what they thought they were doing. The multiple disguises of evil have never been more convincingly portrayed.

The Boys in the Band by William Friedkin treats the theme of homosexuality in an unabashed way, adding another film chapter to the growing documentation on the new sex morality.

Brief Encounter is David Lean's classic film on the domestic triangle situation and its appeal to a bored, suburban wife. The fact that she masters it is due to several complex motivations through all of which seems to run some providential force. It is a Madame Bovary theme with a bittersweet ending whose moral remains engraved in the memory of the viewer. The theme of adultery is also treated in *The Indiscretion of an American Wife, Hot Spell, Strangers When We Meet, Two for the Seesaw, Winning* and *Loving.*

Charly See index for location of discussion in previous chapters.

Luchino Visconti's *The Damned.*

Citizen Kane   See index for location of discussion in previous chapters.

The Damned   Luchino Visconti's film about a wealthy industrial family in 1933 Germany and its gradual decay through intrigue and ambition. The inverse proportion between material power and spiritual vigor has never been more tellingly depicted on the screen.

Le Défroqué is the French film of the mid-1950s that stars Pierre Fresnay as a defrocked priest, cynical and unrepentant. A seminarian who earlier served in the military with him dedicates himself to saving the fallen priest's soul. A powerful, if contrived, scene is the sacrilegious consecration by the *défroqué* of a bucket of champagne in a night club. The attempt to portray the communion of the saints with redemptive sacrifice as the bonding agent between unbeliever and believer has been better portrayed in *La Strada*. Nevertheless, this film has many merits, particularly for a cinematic theology.

The Detective stars Frank Sinatra as a superb example of the secular humanist. Self-sufficient, cautious, and totally committed to women, friends, and the cause of the underdog, Sinatra's detective chooses to fulfill his ideals as he defines them, when he wants to, and on his own terms. He does everything "his way." Sinatra leaves the police force to solve a crime with roots in higher echelons of the city's community. Conscience is working but in a secular, yet still charismatic, way. This film directed by Gordon Douglas demonstrates power's evil grip on weaker men. Regarding deviant behavior, there is a powerful scene of a homosexual brothel. The spiritual temperature of a metropolis is adequately registered, providing a panorama of the liabilities of total secularization.

The Diary of Anne Frank is George Stevens's film of one of the great humanistic documents of this century. The atmosphere of brooding evil in Nazi-occupied Holland does not dampen the ardor of youth. As the Jewish adolescent in hiding with her family, Susan Strasberg embodies the courage of her race. The workings of grace —faith, hope, and charity—are artistically insinuated in this touching movie about one of the less anonymous religious martyrs of the Third Reich.

Diary of a Country Priest   See index for location of discussion in previous chapters.

The Exorcist is a horror classic on Satanology.

Federico Fellini's *Satyricon.*

Fellini Satyricon is an unprecedented pan-optic attempt by the Italian film genius who made *La Dolce Vita* to chronicle in baroque images the degenerate Rome described by Petronius. Rarely has the human record of corruption and of evil found such a faithful stenographer.

Forbidden Games is René Clément's unforgettable motion picture on the authenticity of friendship between two French war orphans. If Christ counseled us to be as little children, then Clément's film demonstrates why. The exposé of adult standards is well drawn when the children tenderly make graves for dead animals with crosses from the village cemetery. The ensuing opposition and furor is typical of a type of traditional mind that fails to see the simplicity of children's deeds. The final scene is one of the most heartbreaking ever filmed, revealing the insensitivity of the grown-up world, so spiritually stunted, so underdeveloped in terms of compassion.

The Fugitive   See index for location of discussion in previous chapters.

The Goddess is a screen version of Paddy Chayefsky's scenario about a sexually provocative movie actress. The film, following closely the life of Marilyn Monroe, awakes compassion in the viewer. The flashback sequence of childhood portrays a puritanical background that provokes the later reaction of permissiveness. As in *Citizen Kane*, *In Cold Blood*, *Wild in the Streets*, and *Midnight Cowboy*, we see the earlier traumas that underlie the protagonist's behavior. Again the "divine scent" seems to be lost, but despite this, Kim Stanley's role indicates an innocence and authenticity that the bustle and glamor of movieland never seem to have corrupted. A cinematic theology interested in the psychology of the prodigal could do no better than to study this film.

The Good Earth is the film of Pearl Buck's best-selling novel starring Paul Muni as a poor Chinese farmer and Luise Rainer as his peasant wife. Temptation, conversion, and fidelity to duty are the theological themes that emerge as Muni becomes wealthy, takes a concubine, forgets his wife, and, following a locust plague, returns, poorer and wiser, to his waiting, forgiving mate. The plague and the moral "black-and-white" emphases convey a genuine Eastern flavor of the Old Testament. How wealth changes the spiritual state of a person is as well delineated here as in *Citizen Kane*.

The Graduate is Mike Nichols's penetrating examination of youth, suburbia, and contemporary university life. Starring Dustin Hoffman, Anne Bancroft, and Katherine Ross, the film superbly illustrates what might be called losing "the divine scent." Everyone is a law unto himself; there is no evidence of the secular humanistic credo of a Bogart, a Newman, a Brando, or a Sinatra. Experience for experience's sake is Benjamin's guiding norm as he ricochets from pity for his suburban parents to infatuation for another man's wife to flight with a lovely Berkeley coed. Whither now? asks the reflective moviegoer. The trail is wide open but one searches vainly for the trailmarkers. The film accurately presents the low threshold of frustration of young people in America with their anxieties and devil-may-care attitudes. That is why it should definitely be seen by those interested in the spiritual future of our "nuclear-space-jet" age generation. In a similar vein are films such as *Darling, Morgan!*, *The Goddess*, *Petulia*, and *Three in the Attic*.

The Great White Hope stars James Earl Jones as the Negro heavyweight boxer who succeeded in humbling "white America" in the pre-World War I era by winning the championship and taking a beautiful white woman as his partner. Human dignity has seldom been maintained so well amid so much adversity. All the more gripping when one recalls that it is the basic outline of Jack Johnson's life.

Greed is Erich von Stroheim's silent film based on Frank Norris's naturalistic novel, *McTeague*. Jean Hersholt and Zazu Pitts act out the wordless plot in a manner at first disconcerting. But the picture gradually absorbs the audience in its story of a dentist and his avaricious wife. Spelled out in bold acting images of a mute morality play, the film provides some interesting questions on personal avarice and cupidity, a theme little discussed in an age of collective status-seeking, national plans for raising per capita income, and capitalization plans of institutions. The welfare-state systems of both socialism and capitalism have replaced the classic passion of greed with the desire for security.

Ikiru See index for location of discussion in previous chapters.

Khartoum is a Cinerama movie plot about British imperialism,

Arab independence, and the meeting of East and West. The religious background is implicit: Christians versus Moslems without any apparent appreciation of their common roots in a revealed religion. Any theology of history must explain how at policy-making levels the logical inferences are not often drawn from the religious premises of belief in the cultures involved. *Khartoum* and *Lawrence of Arabia* provide food for such thoughts. The Mahdi (Laurence Olivier) and Lord Gordon (Charlton Heston) meet, not under a common religious sign, but rather under an antagonistic political one. Only evil seems to be the winner as both sides play the game of intrigue and bloodshed.

La Dolce Vita   See index for location of discussion in previous chapters.

La Strada   See index for location of discussion in previous chapters.

Lilies of the Field   See index for location of discussion in previous chapters.

Limelight is Charlie Chaplin's film on the dedication of an aging vaudeville trouper, Calvaro, to a young ballerina (Claire Bloom) whom he saves from suicide. The film bristles with the subject of love, faith, and hope. If the dancer gives him a reason for living now that his talent is on the decline, then Calvaro is the staff on which she can lean in her movements of insecurity. His death backstage during her performance is the occasion of the rebirth of her self-confidence. Again, as in *Ikiru*, death has no victory, for it was occasioned by selfless attention to another. Just how human and theologically bright this film is can be judged by contrasting it with Chaplin's previous effort (*Monsieur Verdoux*) and his subsequent movie (*King in New York*).

Lonely are the Brave   See index for location of discussion in previous chapters.

Loving is Irvin Kershner's attempt to film a "slice of life" from U.S. suburbia. Alienation, corruption, and psychological "dying" are impeccably conveyed by George Segal as the amoral commuter.

M   See index for location of discussion in previous chapters.

The Magic Christian is black humor at its blackest. Peter Sellers plays Guy Grand, the multimillionaire who proves to himself that everyone has a price. Ringo Starr as his adopted son helps the audience to see through the pious veils of social convention and religious posturing into the moral vacuity of mid-twentieth-century civilization. Joseph McGrath directed.

A Man for All Seasons See index for location of discussion in previous chapters.

The Mark See index for location of discussion in previous chapters.

M*A*S*H* is a fast-paced film about the mobile army surgical hospital near the front lines in Korea. Three young surgeons tax their powers of transcendence to remain sane and human in a situation of absurdity both in medical and military terms. Possesses the same fierce charm as *Midnight Cowboy, Catch 22,* and *The Great White Hope.*

Men of Aran See index for location of discussion in previous chapters.

Midnight Cowboy See index for location of discussion in previous chapters.

The Milky Way is Luis Buñuel's visual attempt to record in his unique way the implications of mystical experience in a religious convent. Debunking and surrealistic indulgences aside, this film touches on the wellsprings of ascetical discipline. It is thus relevant to the themes of grace, death, and charism.

The Miracle Worker is Arthur Penn's film of the Broadway play based on Helen Keller's childhood. As the deaf, dumb, and blind girl locked in the castle of her ego, Patty Duke acts brilliantly opposite Anne Bancroft's Anne Sullivan, the persevering tutor who succeeds in lowering the drawbridge of sign language so that uncivilized Helen might communicate across the moat of her sightless and soundless world. A true humanistic testament, the story offers many parallels to such theological considerations as revelation, (Helen at the water pump, discovering language), victimhood (the humiliations of Anne Sullivan), and redemption (the blossoming of affection in the grateful Helen).

The Misfits is John Huston's unusual film, a parallel between the dying breed of mustangs, now hunted to supply dogfood rather than for riding purposes, and a group of sensitive persons who no longer fit the industrialized, impersonal civilization in which they find themselves. Clark Gable, Marilyn Monroe, Thelma Ritter (all now dead), and Burgess Meredith help make this an interesting film if not a great one. As a contribution toward a sociotheology, it deserves to rank with such Westerns as *Lonely Are the Brave, Hud,* and *Will Penny.*

Monsieur Verdoux   See index for location of discussion in previous chapters.

A Nun's Story is Fred Zinneman's film of a professed sister (Audrey Hepburn) who, after a missionary tour in Africa, has second thoughts about her divine call to a community, traditional and committed to semimedieval practices. The problem is conscience and the difficulty of finding one's path and God's will. Is there such a thing as a temporary vocation? Can leaving a religious order be, as a personal choice, the better thing? When, if ever, does inflexible resistance to modernization exonerate the religious from their responsibilities to a life of dedication in this community? These are the thorny questions that could be posed after viewing *A Nun's Story.*

The Passion of Joan of Arc is Carl Dreyer's memorable silent screen achievement in which Falconetti interprets the role of the soldier maiden burned at the stake at Rouen. Similar to *A Man for All Seasons,* Dreyer's movie is a study in temptation, namely Joan's initial willingness to sign a confession. Later she becomes remorseful, recalling that she must be faithful to her voices even at the price of death. This is grace in all the bloom of martyrdom with the resurrection triumph coinciding with the act of death itself.

Patton is Franklin Schaffner's film on the controversial World War II General who lived the gospel of unconditional surrender. George C. Scott is utterly convincing as the stoic tank commander whom his men ironically nicknamed "Blood and Guts" ("our blood and his guts"). This film should be discussed in terms of the politics of the gospel and teachings on nonviolence.

The Pawnbroker   See index for location of discussion in previous chapters.

The Prime of Miss Jean Brodie   See index for location of discussion in previous chapters.

Rachel, Rachel   Paul Newman's artful direction of Joanne Woodward makes this a telling spiritual document of loneliness in the life of a spinster schoolteacher.

Rashomon is Akira Kurosawa's classic film about the relativism of truth, guilt, and virtue. The unbending dogmatic mind is dealt a powerful blow in this morality play about a bandit who rapes a woman in the presence of her bound husband and then murders him. Testimony varies even though court procedure sifts it carefully. Even in the Gospel's account of Christ's trials before Annas and Caiaphas, the charges, although preconcerted, were conflicting. So in *Rashomon* the audience is given a taste of Oriental wisdom, disposing it to be cautious of human language. Once we know what is in man we are more fearful even of ourselves.

Rebel Without a Cause presents Nicholas Ray's case study of American youth at odds with school, parents, and society in general. James Dean has left us his cameo role, the model of all the world's defiant youth. If *The Graduate* presents Benjamin as an existential "taker," *Rebel Without A Cause* gives us the contrasting existential "nay-sayer." Benjamin is an activist and more Sartrean; Dean's character is pensive and more like Camus. These implicit creeds, important for a behavioral theology, are also discernible in *The Wild One*, *The Leather Boys*, *Look Back in Anger*, *Don't look Back*, *The Entertainer*, and *This Sporting Life*.

Rosemary is a German film directed by Rolf Thiele and based on Erich Kuby's fictionalized account of Rosemary Nitribitt, a Frankfurt prostitute, found strangled in her bathtub with a silk stocking. The clients of Rosemary are among some of Germany's leading architects of the *Wunderwirtschaft*. Having become successful she is drawn into industrial espionage, tape-recording the conversations of her patrons. Her death, still unsolved, is fraught with social, moral, and theological significance. Wealth and comfort disguise the perilous waters in which humans often navigate complacently. This film is much more savage in its prophetic posture than *Citizen Kane*, *The Magnificent Ambersons*, and *The Good Earth*.

Rosemary's Baby features John Cassavetes as the devil incarnate and Mia Farrow as his unsuspecting and pregnant wife. The merit of the film for a cinematic theology is its reflection of the growing interest in Western society for practices such as astrology, seances, and, as we see at the end, the witches' coven to honor Satan. It is Hollywood's attempt at being contemporary and shocking. Though neither purpose really miscarries, the film has none of the eerie conviction of *Day of Wrath, The Crucible, The Seventh Seal, Virgin Spring, Black Orpheus,* or *Seance on a Wet Afternoon.* These films create the sense of diabolic nearness more convincingly than *Rosemary's Baby.*

Sanshiro is an early Kurosawa film about a judo disciple who loses his arrogance as he learns that spiritual control of one's passions is indispensable for even physical feats. The lesson is one that Robert Rossen stresses in showing Paul Newman's growth in self-control as the pool shark in *The Hustler.* If in that film the cue stick was an extension of the player, then in *Sanshiro* judo technique is the message and the judo artist is the medium. The scene where Sanshiro gains Enlightenment through his night-long vigil in the lily pond is one of delicate beauty. Humility is the fundamental attitude for true greatness as Kurosawa reveals that the real judo master, more than an adroit technician, is also master of himself. Ascetic theology brims over throughout this sublime film.

Sergeant York features Gary Cooper as the real-life Quaker recruit who becomes transformed from pacifist to active combatant in the France of World War I. It shows how cultural religion can dilute ideals by an excessively literal interpretation of a popular belief, "My country, right or wrong." A World War II film, designed to inspire patriotism, *Sergeant York* conveys the power of sociological propaganda in converting tradition-oriented believers into secular humanists. It is a study of spiritual alchemy in reverse. Other films about Quaker ethics are *Friendly Persuasion* and *High Noon,* also starring Gary Cooper.

The Seventh Seal　See index for location of discussion in previous chapters.

Shoes of the Fisherman　See index for location of discussion in previous chapters.

Simon of the Desert is Luis Buñuel's movie on the futility of ascetical heroics. In his usual iconoclastic manner, Buñuel unmasks the pretenses of a Father of the Desert, Simon Stylites, the Saint who lived on a pillar. The fanciful abduction of the saint by the devil in the form of a pretty woman further strains credulity when Simon, in Left Bank attire, is seen in a mid-twentieth-century discothèque, serenely watching the swaying hips, the bouncing beads, and the whirling mini-skirts. Buñuel insinuates that all, even the great athletes of God, will grow tepid in the emerging secular world-city of self-interest and the hedonistic calculus.

Targets is Peter Bogdanovich's film based on the true incident of the fanatical ex-Marine who installed himself aloft the University of Texas tower and ambushed 44 people with a rifle. The young lad in the film goes on a similar spree, killing relatives and innocent pedestrians indiscriminately. This testament to violence is an indictment of contemporary urban Western Civilization as is *Blast of Silence, In Cold Blood, The Collector, The Man with the Golden Arm, A Hatful of Rain, Medium Cool,* and *The Night of the Following Day.* In what the sociologist Pitirim A. Sorokin calls "sensate culture" it is difficult to assign guilt, as we saw with individuals such as M, Monsieur Verdoux, the thief in *Pickpocket,* the kidnaper in *High and Low,* and the killer in *Targets.* Who is the victim and who is the victimizer? Again evil becomes so diffuse that one feels that only the demonic forces are the beneficiaries.

They Won't Forget is Mervyn LeRoy's splendid account of race prejudice, crowd fury, and aborted justice in the Deep South. A killing occurs, circumstantial evidence points to a Negro; the prosecuting attorney (Claude Rains) soon discovers evidence to the contrary; the mob clamors for swift justice. Should the accused Negro be given a fair trial? What if he is exonerated? Will the social consequences be far greater than the conviction of his man? While the film leaves unresolved the guilt of the Negro, it is clear that the city officials offer him up as the lesser of two evils. *They Won't Forget* ranks with other excellent films on the loss of reason in crowds and the diabolical intent that can possess them: *Fury, The Ox-Bow Incident, To Kill a Mockingbird, The Long Rope,* and *Maniac.*

2001: Space Odyssey   See index for location of discussion in previous chapters.

Umberto D   See index for location of discussion in previous chapters.

West Side Story is one of Hollywood's most brilliant musical productions, a screen adaptation of the Romeo and Juliet story to Puerto Rican New York. The in-group phenomenon has never been presented more vividly: my girl, my gang, my street, my nationality. Given these unconscious psychological allegiances, the scene is set for the escalation of emotion, hate, and violence. As in Zeffi-relli's *Romeo and Juliet,* so this film also shows how easily Christian people can forget the implications of the nonviolent teachings of Christ.

Wild Strawberries See index for location of discussion in previous chapters.

Wilson See index for location of discussion in previous chapters.

Your Excellency See index for location of discussion in previous chapters.

Z is Costa Gavras's brilliant blending of the best directorial techniques of the sixties to show how the "big knife" of military dictatorship is wielded to cut the roots of socialistic democracy. The film is based on a historical incident in Greece involving a political assassination.

Zabriskie Point is Antonioni's requiem for America as seen through the eyes of a young "uncommitted" couple who must choose to live beyond the pale of law in a personally meaningful relationship or within it in an inauthentic, hypocritical way.

Postface

THE ETYMOLOGICAL root of the words "image" and "imagination" is the same as that of "magic" and "magician." One can infer from this that there is a profound relationship between images and human religious aspirations, that curiosity that primitive peoples try to satisfy through tribal rituals, witch doctors, and practices of magic and superstition. Modern psychoanalysis has concerned itself with images in dreams and wishes. Jung, in particular, has seen the primordial religious urges latent in the "controlling images" of the collective unconscious. As a "compost of heaven and mire," man needs to represent in human, palpable ways the numinous, the transcendental, and the holy. The danger arises, of course, in the human proclivity to mistake the image for the reality it represents. The very first commandment on the Tablets of the Law given to Moses on Mount Sinai proscribed the worship of graven images, whether of clay, wood, stone, ivory, silver, or gold.

Today the images that influence man's memory, imagination, mind, and will are more subtle. In the scientific age, we are less prone to worship totem poles, statuary carvings and temple figurines. Nevertheless, the temptation is still with us to idolize, to believe that one is in touch with the supernatural through some visible or audible link with earth. Contemporary urban man is literally barraged with "images." It has been estimated that the average New York commuter receives some 5,000 audiovisual impressions during a weekday: subway and billboard advertisements, tabloids, pictorial journals, magazines, radio, television, and cinema. Some believe we live in a new "photocivilization" where more and more the image, either still or in motion, is the passport to belief and acceptability. In his film, *Blow-Up*, Antonioni treated this topic of the exaggerated emphasis that photographic credentials have in mid-twentieth-century Western civilization. In fact, the saturation of visual communications may not be an insignificant reason for the emergence of a "God-is-dead" movement in the West and the popularity in the sixties of magical rites such as seances, Black Masses, witchcraft, and devil worship.

While recognizing this danger, this primer on a cinematic theology has sought to establish the positive value of the "image." The film image reflects a world dynamic that, if ambivalent in terms of the clash of good and evil, testifies to the goodness of creation, the abiding presence of Providence, and the ultimate triumph of the God-intoxicated person in sacrifice and martyrdom. If the temptation to idolatry has not been diminished by the advent of the camera, the motion picture screen and the television set, there is still in these products of man's technical genius a yearning to give witness to the deepest aspirations of the human spirit and the larger scheme of truth after which it thirsts. The Bible teaches that Christ is the Image par excellence, reflecting the substance of the Divine Father who sent Him (*Epistle to the Hebrews*:1–3). All images, therefore, have some necessary relation to this Proto-Image, the matrix of the Eternal Plan of Providence. It may be a relation of conscious affirmation of this image; it may be an anonymous allegiance through an honest, if stumbling, search; it may be a rejection through indifference or indolence; or it may be an overt rejection of this image in unconcealed hostility. If the world drama, as Scripture maintains, is theological in essence, then the new world art form of cinema mirrors this world drama as a mystery play with many theological clues.

Notes

Introduction

1. Arnold Hauser, *The Social History of Art* (New York: Random House, Vintage Books, 1951), pp. 243–44.
2. Marshall McLuhan, *The Gutenberg Galaxy* (Toronto: University of Toronto Press, 1962).
3. Lo Duca, *L'Histoire du Cinéma* (Paris: Presses Universitaries de France, 1956), pp. 28–61.
4. Antoine de Saint-Exupéry, *The Little Prince*, trans. Katherine Woods (New York: Penguin Books, 1965), pp. 7–9.
5. Frances Flaherty, "Explorations," in *Film: Book 1*, ed. Robert Hughes (New York: Grove Press, 1959), p. 63.
6. C. S. Lewis, *The Abolition of Man* (New York: Collier Books, 1962), p. 91.
7. Kenneth Boulding, *The Image* (Ann Arbor: University of Michigan Press, 1956), p. 91.
8. Vincent Sheean, "Day of Darkness," *Show*, September 1962, pp. 70–71.
9. *Loc. cit.*
10. *Loc. cit.*
11. "The Universal Magic of the Movies," *Life*, December 20, 1963, p. 13.
12. Jerome S. Bruner, "Myth and Identity," in *Myth and Mythmaking*, ed. Henry A. Murray (New York: George Braziller, 1960), pp. 276–77.

1 Religious Man in Secular Society

1. Herbert Marcuse, *Eros and Civilization* (New York: Random House, Vintage Books, 1955), p. xxii.
2. Harvey Cox, *The Secular City* (New York: The Macmillan Co., 1965), p. 1.
3. J. Robert Oppenheimer, *The Open Mind* (New York: Simon & Schuster, 1963), p. 54.
4. Arthur Knight, *The Liveliest Art* (New York: Mentor Books, 1959), p. 136.
5. A lengthy review of *The Apu Trilogy* can be found in Parker Tyler, *Classics of the Foreign Film* (New York: The Citadel Press, 1962), pp. 226–31. See also Pauline Kael, *I Lost It at the Movies* (Boston: Little, Brown & Co., 1954), pp. 248–49.
6. Karl Polyani, *The Great Transformation* (Boston: Beacon Press, 1957), pp. 43–55.
7. Daniel Keyes, *Flowers for Algernon* (New York: Bantam Books, 1968), p. 173.
8. *Ibid.*, pp. 173–74.
9. Cox, *op. cit.*, pp. 182–91.

2 Man as Inner Center

1. Donald Richie, *The Films of Akira Kurosawa* (Berkeley: University of California Press, 1965), p. 198.
2. Kael, *Kiss Kiss Bang Bang* (New York: Bantam Books, 1969), p. 378.

3 A Cinematic Theology of Freedom

1. Thomas Merton, "The Pasternak Affair," *Thought*, Winter 1959–60, p. 503.
2. Jean Paul Paupert, *The Politics of the Gospel* (New York: Holt, Rinehart & Winston, 1969).
3. Marie Seton, *Sergei N. Eisenstein, A Biography* (New York: A. A. Wyn, 1952), pp. 73–95.
4. Kael, *Kiss Kiss Bang Bang, op. cit.*, p. 447.
5. Tyler, *Classics of the Foreign Films, op. cit.*, p. 47.

4 Conscience, the Transcendental Referee

1. Tyler, *Classics of the Foreign Film, op. cit.,* p. 42.
2. William H. Whyte, Jr., *The Organization Man* (New York: Simon & Schuster, 1956), pp. 245–46.
3. *Ibid.,* p. 400.
4. Gilbert Salachas, "Le Grand Couteau," *Téléciné,* Mars-Avril 1956, p. 4.
5. "Supra-Spy," *Time,* December 24, 1965, p. 34.
6. Kael, *Kiss Kiss Bang Bang, op. cit.,* p. 50.
7. *Loc. cit.*

5 Toward a Cinematic Theology of Sex

1. Donald W. La Badie, "Movies: This Sporting Life," *Show Magazine,* August 1963, p. 25.
2. Jacques Siclier, *Ingmar Bergman* (Paris: Editions Universitaires, 1960), chaps. 2–4.
3. Martin Buber, *I and Thou,* trans. Ronald Gregor Smith (New York: Scribner, 2nd ed., 1958)
4. Vladimir Solovyev, *The Meaning of Love,* trans. Jane Marshall (New York: International Universities Press, 1947).
5. "Movies: Oscar Bound," *Time,* December 24, 1965, p. 32.
6. Merton, "The Pasternak Affair," *op. cit.,* p. 505.
7. Solovyev, *op. cit.,* pp. 66–67.
8. Tyler, *Classics of the Foreign Film, op. cit.,* p. 238.
9. Solovyev, *op. cit.,* pp. 48–61.
10. *Ibid.,* p. 47.
11. "A Plea for Perversion?," *Time,* February 23, 1962, p. 102.
12. Marcuse, *Eros and Civilization, op. cit.,* p. ix.
13. Martha Wolfenstein and Nathan Leites, *Movies: A Psychological Study* (Glencoe, Ill.: The Free Press, 1950).
14. Solovyev, *op. cit.,* p. 53.
15. Erich Fromm, *Die Kunst des Liebens* (Berlin: Ullstin Bücher, 1956), p. 45. The author's translation is based on the quotation of Fromm taken from Karl Marx, *Die Frueh Schriften* (Stuttgart: S. Landshut, 1953), pp. 300 ff.
16. Solovyev, *op. cit.,* p. 55.
17. Marcuse, *op. cit.,* pp. 11 ff.

196

6 A Cinematic Theology of Evil

1. Budd Schulberg, *A Face in the Crowd*, intro. Elia Kazan (New York: Bantam Books, 1957), p. 120.
2. Schulberg, *What Makes Sammy Run?* (New York: The Modern Library, 1952), p. x.
3. "My Lai: An American Tragedy," *Time*, December 5, 1969, pp. 9 ff.
4. See Stephen Scheuer, *Movies on TV* (New York: Bantam Books, 1968), p. 212; Tyler, *Classics of the Foreign Film, op. cit.*, pp. 196–97; and Kael, *Kiss Kiss Bang Bang, op. cit.*, pp. 382–83.
5. "In proportion as the machine industry gained ground, and as the modern concatenation of industrial processes and of markets developed, the conjunctures of business grew more varied and of larger scope at the same time that they became more amenable to shrewd manipulation" (Thorstein Veblen, *The Theory of Business Enterprise* [New York: Mentor Books, 1958], pp. 17–18).
6. Rod Sterling, " 'Patterns' and the Public Image," *People at Work: The Human Element in Modern Business* (New York: American Management Association, Report no. 1, 1957), p. 186.

7 Death on Camera

1. Richie, *The Films of Akira Kurosawa, op. cit.*, p. 86.
2. Edmund Burke, "The Speech to the Electors at Bristol," *The Works of Edmund Burke*, III (London: Oxford University Press, 1907–34), p. 6.
3. Ivor Montagu, "Dovzhenko—Poet of Life Eternal," *Sight and Sound*, Summer 1957, p. 44.
4. Mircea Eliade, *The Sacred and Profane*, trans. Willard R. Trask (New York: Harper & Row, 1961), pp. 147–48.
5. Hauser, *The Social History of Art, op. cit.*, pp. 15–16.
6. Eliade, *op. cit.*, p. 200.
7. Jean Leirens, *Le Cinéma et la Crise de Notre Temps* (Paris: Editions du Cerf, 1960), pp. 2–36.
8. David Riesman, Nathan Glazer, and Reuel Denney, *The Lonely Crowd* (Garden City, N. Y.: Doubleday Anchor Books, 1955), pp. 63–67.
9. This fascinating link between communications, conscience, and rebirth has been carefully explored in Annie Kraus, *Dummheit* (Freiburg: Herder Verlag, 1959).

10. Tyler, *Classics of the Foreign Film, op. cit.*, p. 234.
11. *Loc. cit.*
12. Jacques Siclier, *Ingmar Bergman* (Paris: Editions Universitaires, 1960), pp. 131–32.
13. *Loc. cit.*
14. Henri Agel, *Vittorio de Sica* (Paris, Editions Universitaires, 1955), pp. 128–29.
15. Kael, *Kiss Kiss Bang Bang, op. cit.*, p. 459.
16. *Ibid.*, p. 305.

8   Grace on the Screen

1. Kael, *Kiss Kiss Bang Bang, op. cit.*, p. 196.
2. *Thomas Woodrow Wilson: A Psychological Study* by Sigmund Freud and William Bullitt (Boston: Houghton Mifflin Co., 1967).
3. An excellent appreciative review of this film was written by Moira Walsh in *America*, January 5, 1963, pp. 26–27.
4. Two examples are: Robert Neville, "The Soft Life in Italy," *Harper's*, September 1968, p. 68; and Tyler, *op. cit.*, p. 249.
5. For this interpretation I am indebted to Fr. Nazareno Taddei, S.J., a noted Italian movie critic who has known Fellini for years and has talked with him at length about his work and its spiritual significance.
6. D. T. Suzuki, *Selected Writings of D. T. Suzuki: Zen Buddhism*, ed. William Barrett (Garden City, N. Y.: Doubleday Anchor Books, 1956), p. xvi.
7. A full-length account of *Red Beard* is to be found in Richie, *The Films of Akira Kurosawa, op. cit.*, pp. 171–83.
8. *Ibid.*, pp. 172–73.
9. *Ibid.*, p. 175.
10. Raymond Durgnat, "Diary of a Country Priest," *Films and Filming*, December 1966, pp. 31–32.

9   The Screen's Theology of Sacrificial Love

1. Joseph M. Duffy, Jr., "The Lost World of Graham Greene," *Thought*, Summer 1958, pp. 229–30.
2. John Mitry, *John Ford* (Paris: Editions Universitaires, 1954), pp. 82–83.
3. This film is reviewed in Tyler, *Classics of the Foreign Film, op. cit.*, pp.

198

202–5, and in Kael, *Kiss Kiss Bang Bang, op. cit.*, p. 313.

4. See an excellent review, Gilbert Salachas, "Celui qui Doit Mourir," *Téléciné*, August-September, 1957, pp. 2–11.
5. Durgnat, "Luis Buñuel," *Diary of a Country Priest, op. cit.*, pp. 109–12.
6. Leirens, *Le Cinéma et la Crise de Notre Temps, op. cit.*, p. 67.
7. Kael, *Kiss Kiss Bang Bang, op. cit.*, p. 162.

10   A Cinematic Theology of the Future

1. Keyes, *Flowers for Algernon, op. cit.*
2. *Ibid.*, p. 88.
3. *Ibid.*, p. 172.
4. *Ibid.*, p. 176.
5. *Ibid.*, p. 172.
6. Eugene Burdick and Harvey Wheeler, *Fail-Safe* (New York: Dell, 1962), preface.
7. *Ibid.*, p. 278.
8. *Ibid.*, p. 280.
9. There is a lengthy review of this film in Kael, *Kiss Kiss Bang Bang, op. cit.*, pp. 179–84.
10. A brief adverse review of this film appears in Scheuer, *op. cit.*, p. 76.
11. William F. Nolan, ed., *The Pseudo-People* (New York: Berkeley Medallion Books, 1965).
12. Isaac Asimov, "Evidence," in *ibid.*, p. 105.
13. C. S. Lewis, *The Abolition of Man, op. cit.*, p. 72.

11   Teaching Theology Through Cinema

1. McLuhan, *The Gutenberg Galaxy, op. cit.*, p. 216.
2. *Ibid.*, p. 217.
3. Andrew Sarris, "The Farthest-Out Moviegoers," *Saturday Review*, December 26, 1964, pp. 14–15.
4. Hollis Alpert, "Now the Earlier, Earlier Show," *The New York Times Magazine*, August 11, 1963, pp. 22, 23, 38.

Index of Directors and Films

70 71 72 73 10 9 8 7 6 5 4 3 2 1